fried butter

fried butter

A FOOD MEMOIR

ABE OPINCAR

SOHO

With one exception, the chapters all appeared previously in the San Diego *Reader* under the pseudonym of Max Nash.

Published by
Soho Press, Inc.
853 Broadway
New York, NY 10003
www.sohopress.com

Library of Congress Cataloging-in-Publication Data

Opincar, Abe, 1961–
Fried butter : a food memoir / Abe Opincar.
p. cm.
ISBN 1-56947-334-X (alk. paper)
1. Opincar, Abe, 1961– —Biography. 2. Cookery, International.
I. Title.

TX649.O63A3   2003
641.59—dc21

2002042911

10   9   8   7   6   5   4   3   2   1

For my father and for my brother,
may their memory be always for blessing.

I thank Claudia, Cristina, Devorah, Doina, Ernesto,
Esteban, Keo, Matitiyahu, Ron, Sophie, and Teresa,
for their ideas and memories, and for helping me
clarify my own.

I thank my publisher and my editor at
the *San Diego Reader*, Jim Holman and
Judith Moore, for encouraging me.

And I thank Juris Jurjevics—*tu esi patiess labs draugs*.

"Ezra the Scribe decreed that men should eat garlic on Sabbath eve. Rabbi Shlomo Yitzchaki explained that God commanded man and wife to make love on Sabbath eve, and that garlic increases sexual desire. Other rabbis have said that garlic satisfies hunger, warms the body, makes the face radiant, and increases sexual desire. Other rabbis have said that garlic creates love and does away with jealousy."

—BABYLONIAN TALMUD, BABA KAMA 82A

chapter one

I BAKED A CHICKEN the night I left my wife. It was a chubby-thighed roasting hen I rubbed with olive oil and salt and hefted into a 500-degree oven where I left it to sizzle for about an hour. The hen's buttery smell filled the kitchen. Soup I'd made with the hen's neck, giblets, and feet simmered on the stove. Out in the dining room, two guests, my wife, my stepson and his wife, chattered and laughed and complained they were hungry. Our Sabbath candles shone in their silver holders. The challah waited beneath its embroidered velvet cover to be blessed.

On Friday nights we gathered around that big oak table where I blessed my stepson and his wife, where I sang *Aishes Chayil* to my wife ("Who might find a woman of valor? Her value is far beyond pearls. . . ."), where I blessed wine and bread, served chicken soup, carved juicy hens, chanted the Grace After Meals ("Blessed are You, our God, King of the Universe, who nourishes the entire world, in His goodness, with grace, with kindness, and with mercy. . . .") For a long while I thought my life was full and sweet. For a while it was.

"He monopolized my time on my honeymoon," is what my wife told Star and Bob, our marriage counselors, by way of expressing her past and present dissatisfactions. I sat there and wondered about my wife's use of the possessive, "*my* honeymoon." But what did I know? I wasn't sure of much. The only thing I knew for certain was that I was paying $185 an hour to a husband-and-wife team named Star and Bob to listen to my wife complain that I'd monopolized her time on her honeymoon.

"Interesting," murmured Star, toying with her chunky ethnic necklace. Bob picked imaginary lint off his taupe corduroys. Star, eyes wide with bland compassion, turned to me. "What are you feeling?"

"I'm feeling," I said, "that I have to go home and bake a chicken."

I suppose every failed marriage has its own Dealey Plaza, Texas School Book Depository, grassy knoll. Its own Star and Bob. A mystery point where fatigue, despair, and anger find triangulation. Motives forever remain murky; history changed nonetheless. When I left Star and Bob's office, I knew I would never come back.

I went home and monopolized a roasting hen's time. As millions of Jews have done for centuries on early Friday evenings, I baked a chicken. Humming "Some Enchanted Evening," my wife cleaned the living room. She arranged daisies in a vase. The sun went down. She lighted and blessed two candles. The guests arrived and, a few minutes later, my stepson and his wife. Our meal began.

God created the Sabbath and said, "Israel shall be your mate." Rabbis further explained, "Accordingly, every week, Israel greets the Sabbath like a groom awaiting his bride." The Sabbath, too, represents a foretaste of Heaven, a never-ending honeymoon. I didn't want our meal to end. I wanted it to go on forever.

Our guests said good-bye. My stepson and his wife lingered. She got up and hugged me. "You're the father I always wished I'd have." She wasn't going to wish that for much longer.

They left. The house was quiet. My wife cleared the table, then went to bed. I fed the dog and went outside and stared at the garden I planted. Every seed I'd carelessly poked into the ground, every sunflower, every bean, every marigold, every gourd, every mint, every tomato, had shot up out of the earth. The tiny one- and two-leafed sprouts mocked me.

I crept back to the bedroom to take some clothes, a book I was reading, a leather satchel. My wife was asleep. Under the reading lamp, her long dark curls, her sweet pale complexion, glowed. Her lips were slightly parted. I wanted to kiss them again. I wanted to taste her breath again. I knew I could never make her happy.

The last time I saw it, our dining room was chilly. The candles in their silver holders flickered. (You don't blow Sabbath candles out.) Our dog, an aging black Labrador, snoozed beneath the table. In the kitchen, the refrigerator hummed.

I took the leftover baked chicken with me and ate it in my motel room the next afternoon for lunch.

MY PARENTS SENT ME to school in France when I was fifteen. The French family I lived with, the Rampillons, owned a large estate in the wine country outside Bordeaux. Former colonials, they'd migrated to France after Moroccan independence in 1956, and, like many former colonials, were touchy about their place in French society. They were well educated. They had money. But to the wine country's stuffy old families, they were outsiders. The Bordeaux region is known in France for its conservatism. To assuage their insecurity, the Rampillons seized upon the conventions and manners of Bordeaux's upper-middle-class as only true outsiders could. The Rampillons' Sunday lunches filled me with dread.

I couldn't have been more primitive if I'd crossed their threshold on all fours. I was from Southern California, which to the Rampillons was as faraway and exotic as Borneo. I think they invited me into their home in the same spirit as those families who adopt chimps in the hopes of teaching them sign language. They were at first charmed by my rudimentary attempts at communication, but it soon became clear that I lacked even the most basic skills to participate in bourgeois domestic life. I once appeared barefoot in the television room. Arching an eyebrow, Madame Rampillon pointed at my naked feet and said, "*Franchement, je trouve ça très sale.*" Frankly, I find that very dirty.

From then on I went barefoot only when I bathed.

There is perhaps no better environment for learning a foreign language than one of intimidation and fear. A mistake made once is not one you're likely to make twice. The Rampillons were determined to civilize me and as Frenchmen they believed there was no higher mark of civilization than the correct use and pronunciation of the French language. Even the maids and groundskeepers were enlisted in this effort, although Monsieur Rampillon warned I would do best not to imitate their accents. While in the Rampillon home, or on the acres of land surrounding it, I could not open my mouth without hearing five or six strident voices barking out corrections. If I made grammatical mistakes while asking the cook for an afterschool snack, she reported them to Madame Rampillon who, later in the evening, made sure they did not go uncorrected. Even guests *chez Rampillon* were invited to polish my use of the subjunctive.

During meals, speaking good French while minding bourgeois table manners was as simple as simultaneously playing a violin and tuba. The Rampillons tried to be patient, but they were faced with someone who did not know that one must never use a knife on any food—with the exception of bread—that has a crust.

My knife was poised above a slice of quiche when Monsieur Rampillon glared at me. "You insult the cook. You are implying that the crust is too hard to cut with your fork." My table manners improved while I was with the Rampillons. I also lost weight.

After months of strict training, when I could finally be depended upon not to use a knife on my quiche, or laughably mispronounce words like *serrurier*, locksmith, the Rampillons decided it was safe to invite an important guest to Sunday lunch. He was, I remember, a widely traveled and elderly professor of agriculture. To show off, I suppose, their success in exotic animal husbandry, the Rampillons seated me next to him. Before us lay the impressive Sunday lunch table: damask tablecloth, antique crystal, sterling silver, the best Bordeaux wines. The lunch at first went well. I embarrassed no one. The professor chatted with me about Southern California. "Your young American," the professor said to Madame and Monsieur Rampillon, "speaks French well." They beamed.

The meal, of course, had to end with fresh fruit and the maid brought peaches to the table. Everyone around me steadied their peaches with their forks and, with simple finesse, began to peel them with their fruit knives. I stared at my peach as if it were a live grenade. Peeling a peach with knife and fork was one trick the Rampillons had not taught me.

God may protect children and drunks, but He's careless with young Americans in France. The late-spring peaches weren't very ripe. I jabbed a fork at mine and even now I can see it hop from my plate and roll, as if guided by an unseen malevolent force, toward the professor's red wine glass. There was something obscenely inevitable about my direct hit, about the way the crystal exploded when it fell, the way the dark red wine surged onto the white tablecloth. In my mind I've replayed the scene thousands of times. For me, the peach and wine glass have lost none of their sick fascination.

The French often do have beautiful manners. No one laughed. No one stared. No one stopped the flow of conversation. The professor simply tossed his napkin over the mess. Monsieur Rampillon called the maid in from the kitchen. "I believe our young American would perhaps prefer a banana."

chapter two

M Y NEIGHBOR ARLENE, a grave older woman who drives a Trans Am, leaves sacks of persimmons by my front door. The trees in her backyard are so heavy with fruit their branches bend low to the ground. In the late afternoon blue jays mass in the branches. Bright orange pulp shines on their beaks. I stand in the alley, watching the feast. "Hey, leave those trees alone!" I shout, wave my arms. The blue jays ignore me.

Arlene's generosity is one way I know time has passed. Living alone, the days run together. I can give a general outline of my life, but can offer few specific dates. When I come home and find a sack of persimmons by my front door, I know it must be mid-October. I stack the persimmons on the windowsill above the kitchen sink. In a few days they'll begin to soften.

In my unexpected bachelorhood, I tend my garden carefully. I mulch. I weed. I fertilize. I search catalogs for mints, sunflowers, unusual tomatoes. I ignore descriptions of fig trees and lemons, plum trees, apricots, persimmons. Of all the things I could grow, fruit trees would be the most wonderful. But fruit trees take years of care before they mature. I am rootless. I don't know where I might be a few seasons from now.

Arlene doesn't weed much, or mulch, nor does she often water. She tells me she planted her oldest persimmon twenty years ago. "But the two others were volunteers. They grew from seeds blue jays dropped to the ground. They came up just like that. Now they make more persimmons than I know what to do with."

She sometimes talks to me over our backyard fence while I weed and fuss with my lawn. She talks about her children. She seems to have several. There are grandchildren. I can never keep track. They rarely visit, at any rate. She doesn't seem to mind.

"You can raise 'em," she says, "but you can't live their lives for 'em. You do the hard work, then let 'em go."

She guesses her persimmons are the domestic American variety, *Diospyros virginiana*. I don't agree. American persimmons are round. Arlene's come to a point. I think they might be Hachiya persimmons, one of the Japanese varieties. Until ripe, they are, like American persimmons, puckery, astringent. In the morning while I make coffee I give the persimmons on the window ledge a little squeeze. They ripen from the inside out. The trick is to wait until they're soft inside, custardlike. They're very sweet and, to me, taste a little like pumpkin. This waiting, the watchfulness required, makes me think they're an old-fashioned pleasure. Persimmons are a patient fruit.

My mother comes to visit. I find her one afternoon parked before the kitchen sink, a half-eaten persimmon in one hand.

"When I was a little girl," she says, "we lived near a persimmon grove. I remember climbing up into the trees and eating all I wanted. Mother would say, 'Don't do that, you'll make yourself sick.' And I did make myself sick. I never listened."

She looks at me. "You always listened. You were a good kid. Before your father died he said that if he'd known they would have turned out just like you, we would have had more children."

Lately, she's given to that sort of introspection. My dead father. Her dead mother. My childhood. Nearly seventy years old, she sleeps deeply throughout the night. I hear her snore and murmur. In the early evenings she makes long phone calls to my nine-year-old nephew. She talks to him about school. She helps him with his math.

"That little boy is devoted to me," she says. "I don't know what I'd do without him."

In an offhand way she asks if I'll ever marry again. I say I doubt it. She changes the subject, picks up her needlepoint—a fat green toad crouched on a lily pad.

"Your father always wanted to bounce a child of yours on his knee."

The next day Arlene brings more persimmons. My mother meets her at the door. The two start to talk, to laugh. Both of them widows, unwilling survivors. I excuse myself and take out the trash. Dust blows down the unpaved alley. A dozen blue jays perch atop my weather-beaten fence. The birds look at me, then at Arlene's persimmons. In a rush of twitterings and chirps, they descend upon the fruit, or what's left of it. Half-eaten persimmons dangle forlornly amid the brown and red leaves. I start to chase the blue jays away, but I stop. There will be more than enough persimmons next year, I figure. And the year after.

I WAS PLANTING BASIL in a new raised bed when the radio announced that cheese would kill me. A nutritionist, her voice tinny and nasal on my cheap radio, explained how cheese lined arteries with "gluelike" cholesterol, leading to "premature aging and death." She talked about growth hormones, about insecticides in cattle feed. She said Americans had to "pay attention to what they ate, or face the consequences." I turned off the radio and watered my basil.

Before dawn on the full-moon day of the Hindu month Ashwini, women in rural India offer camphor, water, rice, and flowers to the basil plant in their courtyards. The women prostrate themselves before the plant. They sing hymns. In Hindi this particular species, *Ocimum sanctum*, is called Tulsi, the name of a goddess, wife to Vishnu, the Creator. To the devout Hindu, basil doesn't merely symbolize Tulsi, but is the goddess in physical form.

"O Goddess Tulsi," the women pray. "You who are the most precious of Vishnu, you who live according to His Divine Laws, I beseech you to protect the lives of my family and the spirits of those who have died. Hear me, O Goddess."

At ritual's end, the women eat a few leaves, linking basil's flavor with Tulsi, her great mercy, what she promises—loyalty, protection, righteousness. Throughout India, a basil leaf is placed in the mouths of the dying to insure safe conduct to the afterlife.

I've been told that in Iran mothers plant basil on the graves of sons, a symbol of mourning. Today's Iranians in part descend from the Aryans, the same nomadic people who invaded the Indian subcontinent 3500 years ago, bringing with them the gods and hymns that evolved into Hinduism. The Iranian mother who plants basil on her son's grave may be indulging in an old ritual that she, as a Muslim, might otherwise consciously reject.

In my garden I plant many kinds of *Lamiace*, the family to which basil belongs. I like this family—mint, lavender, oregano, thyme, sage, basil—not only because they're fragrant, but also because they're so varied it's sometimes difficult to tell they're related. I imagine their lineage stretching back thousands of years, to a common ancestor, the Mother of All Basil, the Matriarch of Mint, a bushy hardy plant that smelled like heaven.

As I work my garden, I listen to my radio, to California call-in shows that often as not concern health and longevity. Each week brings a new revelation. Leafy green vegetables, it turns out, don't protect against breast cancer. Soy bean products, it turns out, may cause cancer. Or maybe not. The jury's still out. At any rate, honey and garlic nourish beneficent bacteria in the gut.

"I've been eating tofu to prevent menopause," a caller tells the talk-show doctor. "But it gives me indigestion."

The talk-show doctor sighs. "If tofu makes you sick, don't eat it."

Basil is a favorite of newspaper food columnists. Every spring they recite the quaint lore: ancient Greeks believed basil bred scorpions; ancient Romans fed basil to livestock to increase fertility; medieval gardeners thought sniffing basil caused worms "like scorpions" to grow in the brain; basil symbolized wantonness; basil symbolized chastity; Italians cursed basil seed to make sure it grew well.

The woman who sells me herb seedlings is, like most plant professionals I know, thin and strange and practical. Mention Hindu basil rites to her, or Greek scorpions, and she doesn't feign interest for long. I call and tell her I've tried to grow *Ocimum sanctum* from seed and have had no luck. She says she has three young plants she'd be happy to sell me. But I'd better come soon because dark clouds are moving into her part of the county. "You can come up here and stand around in the rain if you want," she says. "But I'm sure as hell not."

I make the drive north to her nursery, forty-five minutes from my home. Lightning rakes the afternoon sky. Hail hits my windshield. A "Closed" sign stands in the herb nursery's driveway, but I drive past it. I find the herb woman in one of her greenhouses, pulling aphids from mint with her finger-nails. She sells me her three Tulsi basils. Marble-size hail strikes the greenhouse roof. Hundreds of little round shadows bounce off its translucent white surface. The sound deafens. We shout at each other. We are inside a drum on which an indifferent storm beats.

WHEN MY MOTHER WAS pregnant with me, her eyes became light sensitive. Cloudless August made her head throb. Sunlight off our bright white garage gave her vertigo. Eggs, she says, fried sunny-side up, barely firm, soothed her stomach. She pulled down all the shades, closed all the curtains. All summer long she sat in the dark kitchen, eating eggs, their yolks shining like little suns on her plate. While she was carrying me, she says, the kitchen smelled always of fried butter.

This past summer the European Centre for Taste Science in Dijon, France, published a study in which pregnant mothers who ate anise seed gave birth to babies who, in their first four days of life, turned toward anise odor. Babies whose mothers didn't eat anise turned away from the odor or ignored it. There are few foods I enjoy more than sunny-side up or soft-boiled eggs, their yolks hot, smooth, and runny.

My mother's job was to care for my brother, father, and me. My retrograde childhood was privileged. My mother made my bed, washed the sheets and pillow cases. She woke me in the morning. I put on clothes she had bought, washed, and ironed. I sat at the breakfast table and she placed before me a plate of eggs cooked just as I liked them. She made the lunch I took to school. She made my after-school snack. She never complained. Once when I was very young she was standing at the kitchen sink washing dishes. I said I wanted to go outside and play. She said, "I'm lonely. Please stay with me and talk." I didn't.

Some foods we take from the world by force. Others, like eggs, seem freely given. Humans, forever hungry, always looking for a handout from brutal stingy Nature, concentrate not upon the hen, but the egg. The hen clucks and blinks and deposits yet another in her nest. Her selflessness is inexplicable, almost comical. The egg is revered as a symbol of eternal life. Its roundness, the endless regularity of its production, suggest the cycle of birth and death. Its brittle shell suggests life's fragility.

That eggs are a feminine food is made obvious in their preparation, which often requires maternal care. Milk is churned and scalded, but eggs, like babies, are "coddled." When discussing soufflés, cookbooks sound like Dr. Spock's *Baby Book*. Kitchen becomes nursery. Whites and yolks must be *carefully* separated. Egg whites must be *gently* folded. Once the soufflé goes into the oven, no loud noises or heavy footsteps! *Shh. Be quiet. Baby's sleeping*.

My mother never taught me to cook. She never let me, my brother, or father, so much as wash dishes. (She feared we wouldn't do it right, that we wouldn't rinse them properly. There was also a generalized fear of germs, and men, she felt, were careless about them.) Even today she regards my cooking as a reckless habit, something I'd be wise to leave in the hands of a wife, if only I were sensible enough to remarry. When she visits she disinfects my sink, scrubs my cutting boards with bactericidal soap. She eyes my refrigerator as if it were booby-trapped. "Have you checked any expiration dates lately?"

When she visits, she cooks for me. I get up in the morning, I smell coffee. I get out of the shower, I smell eggs. I sit at the table, she watches me eat. "You're slumping," she says. Or, "Your nose and forehead look like your father's." I kiss her cheek. She smiles and sighs. She tells me that she'll wash the dishes.

Later in the day she goes out for a while. She returns heavy-laden with groceries. Organic fruit. Organic milk. Whole wheat bread. Organic eggs from free-range hens. She says they have "more vitamins." I tell her I'm not malnourished. She shrugs. She puts the groceries away. She wipes each egg with a damp paper towel and places it in the refrigerator's special holder.

In fourth grade I had my first course in, as it was called back then, sex education. In the darkened classroom, the movie projector stuttered and chattered, dust motes shining in its unsteady beam. *The Miracle of Life* was revealed to us. Sperm, their tails whipping jerkily, mechanically, looked like insects. When the most valiant sperm, twitching in spasms, drilled its way into the passive egg, I felt numb. How could it be that these stupid, speechless, buglike things, acting only on instinct, produced human beings? How could a miracle be so ugly?

Every year on my birthday my mother calls early early in the morning to say, "This is the exact time when you were born." Her tone is cheerful, but she sounds like she can't half believe it. That it happened. That so many years have passed so quickly. I ask if it was all worth it. The pain, the diapers, the breakfasts, the laundry. "I didn't do any of it because I enjoyed it," she says. "I did it out of love."

chapter three

M Y WIZENED AUNT MIRIAM now ekes out her life in a hospital bed in southern Oregon. Only the most primitive part of her brain functions. Her pruney face is expressionless. She is fed through a tube in her upper left abdomen. Every winter she gets pneumonia and every winter she survives. Most everyone agrees that her end began the afternoon she threw a plate of cornmeal mush at my father.

Miriam, with dark olive skin and silky black hair, had been lovely when young. By the time I as a child first met her, she had a faint mustache that repulsed me, and she had lived for decades in mourning. The great love of her life, her husband Andrei, a tailor, died eight years into their marriage. Childless and loyal, she never remarried. She diverted her love toward her brothers, to their children, and to cooking. She was dedicated to Romanian food.

Mamaliga, cornmeal mush, is the Romanian staple. Sometimes made with cheese, it's cooked until firm, then turned out of the pot and onto a platter where it sits, a steamy, golden dome, in the middle of the table. Traditionally, it's sliced with a thread: almost all Romanians, who are particular about such things, prefer their *mamaliga* firm. Andrei, Miriam's late husband, preferred it soft, like grits. My father, confronted with his sister's *mamaliga*, would grunt and say, "Miriam was never the same after she married Andrei."

At least once a week Miriam came to our house to cook. She stood at my mother's stove, one hand on her bony hip, her graying bun coming undone, and stirred cast-iron pots of heavy Romanian food. She wrestled chickens cooked with cabbage into and out of the oven. In sweet butter she fried little Romanian pancakes filled with jam or sour cream. Our faces shined with sweat when we ate Miriam's solid cooking.

When my mother and father retired they decided that Miriam would go live with them in a home they'd bought in southern Oregon. She was getting old, they said. She had no one to take care of her. For a while, things went OK. As her contribution to the household, Miriam did all the cooking. My mother gained weight. My father did, too. Miriam began cooking more and more, spending longer hours in the kitchen.

"We had to buy a freezer," my mother whispered during a late-night phone call from Oregon. "And it's almost full. She makes *mamaliga* for lunch *and* dinner. She won't stop cooking."

My father added, "Miriam puts the 'mania' in Romania."

Finally, one afternoon, he insulted her *mamaliga*. He said he couldn't eat another bite of her "glop." And Miriam, this diminutive woman who'd never uttered a harsh word in her life, cursed my father in Romanian and picked up the plate of "glop" and hurled it at him.

"It hit the wall behind me," explained my father. "And it slid down just like custard. If it had been *real mamaliga*, it would have stuck like glue, plate and all."

Miriam went downhill fast. A few weeks later she took my family's photo albums and with a razor blade cut my father's face out of all the pictures. My mother caught her red-handed, holding dozens of tiny cutouts of my father's smiling face. Several months later, Miriam ran away. My parents called the sheriff. She was found crouched, incoherent, behind a Dumpster in a convenience store parking lot. That night she woke my mother at 3:00 a.m. "Come with me," she said. "There's something I have to show you."

She led my mother outside, through the garden, and down stone steps to the shallow river that ran behind my parents' house. Pointing at the rushing dark water, Miriam said to my mother, "See. This is where you took me after you killed me.

You killed me and you threw my body into the river." My mother started to cry. ("Do you think she'd read my mind?" my mother, exhausted, later asked me.)

Miriam has been demented now for more than a decade. For several years, before she lapsed into her perpetual catnap, she was violent. She bit nurses. She threw handfuls of her own shit. She jumped up and down, trampoline-style, on her hospital bed. Her stamina amazed everyone. She had to be restrained. She's outlived my father and her two other brothers.

My mother still visits her, makes the long drive up to the private facility surrounded by tall pines. There, in the clean white room, my mother strokes Miriam's forehead and talks to her about the weather. Not long ago, while going through family pictures, my mother found one of Andrei and took it with her when she visited Miriam.

"Look, look," said my mother, holding the picture close to Miriam's face. "It's Andrei. I found a picture of Andrei."

My aunt's eyes fluttered open, blinked, struggled to focus. She groaned, my mother said, and with great difficulty bent her head forward to the picture and gently, very softly, kissed it.

I POUR OLIVE OIL into a pan. When the oil is hot I sprinkle into it a tablespoon of turmeric. The yellow powder bubbles and darkens. I crack two eggs into the pan. When the yolks are barely firm, I slide the eggs onto a plate and pour the leftover oil on top. With pita bread I sop up runny yolk and mustardy yellowish oil. There are few moments when I'm happier. Such a simple thing can be enough.

In my odd little immigrant neighborhood everyone knows turmeric. My Indian landlord calls it *haldi* and tells me it's the principal ingredient in curry powder. Patting his big firm belly with both hands, my landlord says "*Haldi* is quite good for the digestion." The Vietnamese woman next door calls it *nghe*. She says she sometimes makes *nghe* tea, which she claims beautifies her skin. Three blocks away the crabby Chinese herbalist, who has always disliked me, sits in his store and scowls when I walk into his shop. He calls turmeric *wong geung*. He refuses to tell me how it's used in China. The earnest shopkeeper at the Ethiopian market tells me that in his country turmeric is *erd* and is used in a sauce for chicken. The Palestinian owner of the Middle Eastern grocery tells me that in Arabic turmeric is *curcoom*, or in slang *arosh*, which means "yellowish." In the Middle East, as throughout Southeast Asia, turmeric is used to make yellow rice, a symbol of celebration.

Although turmeric is native to India, Marco Polo found it in China where he declared it a reasonable substitute for saffron. Eight hundred years later American and British scientists have discovered that turmeric may be a reasonable substitute for the steroids used to treat arthritis. Curcumin, the chemical compound that gives turmeric its intense yellowness, acts as a powerful anti-inflammatory. Research has also shown that curcumin seems to trick cancer cells into killing themselves. In one study, smokers with mouth cancer, after taking curcumin daily for nine months, saw their lesions disappear. Other studies are investigating curcumin's use in the treatment and prevention of colon and breast cancer. The British press now and again runs stories about "Curry: The New Wonder Drug."

Turmeric, a rhizome, in its fresh state looks like a smaller, scruffier version of ginger, a close relative. Cardamom, a ginger cousin, with its pungent eucalyptus-like aroma, evokes Vick's Vap-o-Rub, childhood bronchitis, my mother, and also the Middle East, where cardamom is added to coffee. Turmeric is neither minty-cool like cardamom, nor spicy-hot like ginger. Turmeric powder, the form in which it's most commonly available, has a rough, slightly bitter astringency, like mustard.

I sometimes find fresh turmeric in Vietnamese and Lao markets. Cut open the small, nubby rhizome and its interior is a brilliant carroty orange. Taste a sliver and you understand every caution you've ever heard about fresh herbs versus dried, about the impossibility of translating poetry. Fresh turmeric's flavor takes a while to bloom on the tongue: a strong and pleasant floweriness gives way to a complicated piney, peppery taste. Turmeric powder gives only a dim, inaccurate hint of the real fresh thing.

Last week I was reading a book of Paul Celan's poems translated from German. In the translator's notes he mentions that when translating one poem, the poem I happened to like best, he used "daydream" instead of "dream" for rhythm's sake. But a daydream isn't a dream. I felt I couldn't trust a single line in the book. I doubted that I'd truly understood any of the poems at all. Ethnic cookbooks often offer similar betrayals.

"If you can't get fresh lemon grass," one Thai cookbook assures me, "the dried kind works just as well. If you can't find that, use dried lemon peel."

I add a tablespoon of grated fresh turmeric to boiling water. I stir in a cupful of rice and place the snug lid onto the pot. The kitchen fills with the smell of fresh turmeric. The phone rings. A friend engages me in a discussion about romance. We disagree. I wait for my rice to be done. My friend tells me that I've never truly been in love, that I've only been in love with the idea of being in love.

This isn't the sort of thing I like to listen to while making dinner. I make an excuse. I hang up. I spoon fluffy bright yellow rice onto a plate. I've made plenty of rice with dried turmeric, and like it just as well, but its taste is entirely different. While I eat my rice and baked chicken, I wonder if my friend was right. I've *thought* I was in love. I've *felt* I was in love. Maybe there's a deeper, tenderer, more vivid love that I can't experience or have never found. My messy bachelor's kitchen is quiet. I hear water drip from faucet into sink. I think I have been in love. It may not have been the real thing, but it was close enough.

chapter four

RAIN AND WAITING COME to mind whenever I taste black radishes. They're not a sunny vegetable. They prefer wet cool climates and turn pithy if left in the ground when the weather turns hot. They are stubbornly northern European and my own introduction to them was made in Paris, a city muffled much of the year by low clouds.

It was during a particularly cloudy winter when a woman friend and I, rain stinging our faces, trudged down the Eleventh Arrondissment's narrow black sidewalks to Sophie's apartment for dinner. My friend had known Sophie since childhood. Sophie lived in one of the quarter's ancient court-yards, tucked off a main street, entered through a massive wooden door. Some courtyards in the quarter are straightfor-ward, others are warrenlike, but all were designed to accom-modate the lives of artisans. Workshops on the ground floors. Apartments above. Because these courtyards are tall and nar-row, they are often dark. Moss on cobblestones, ivy on walls.

Sophie's marriage was unhappy. She was from a noble French family, had neither education nor occupation, and had married an artist, a burly Norman with enormous hands and feet who drank and womanized. With his enormous Norman hands, he had transformed their second-floor courtyard apartment into a cozy bohemian home. The apartment's only irreparable flaw was its old wooden floor, which sloped noticeably to the east, giving the rooms a disorienting fun-house aspect. Sophie and her brutish husband had produced a fussy moon-faced baby whose toys—balls, cars, wagons—always rolled away from him down this slanted wooden floor, which had probably something to do with his fussiness and frustration.

Just as the moon-faced baby lived with toys forever escap-ing his reach, Sophie lived with a husband who forever threat-ened to escape hers. Many nights my woman friend and I sat with Sophie at her large oak dinner table, hewn, built, and pol-ished by her Norman lout. While the baby screeched and scrambled after his runaway toys, Sophie, teary-eyed, filled our glasses with Burgundy wines and wondered aloud when and if her husband would come home. Some nights, after waiting one, sometimes two, hours, we would hear his big wet boots thumping up the stairs. Other nights, we would not. My friend tolerated these delayed dinners out of sisterly solidarity for Sophie. I tolerated them because Sophie was a good cook.

Sophie's fatalism unnerved me. I couldn't understand why she didn't snatch up her moon-faced baby and flee to her family's Burgundian château where her mother did needlepoint and flirted with the most extreme factions of reactionary Roman Catholicism. Sophie's mother had taught her how to cook, and to me a rural life, religious extremism aside, would have been better for the baby. Sophie would hear none of it. She preferred her Parisian life to the château's leaky roof and drafty bedrooms. Besides, she said, she'd never leave her husband. She never did. He left her.

On those nights we sat and waited with her, she always set on the table thin slices of black bread she bought at a Polish delicatessen, and a crock of what she called "*radis noir*," black radish, which she had grated and mixed with sour cream. She'd butter the bread and spoon some radish on top and, with a sniffle, hand it to us saying, "*C'est bon pour le foie.*" "It's good for your liver." We sniffled, too. Black radish is almost as strong as horseradish—the French often confuse the two, calling black radish *raifort* rather than *radis noir*. Sophie knew the difference. Her black radish and sour cream kept our stomachs from growling while the smell of her roast *poulet de Bresse*, or her *blanquette de veau* wafted our way from the kitchen.

Sophie taught me how to make black radish. "Don't substitute low-fat, or even whole-milk, yogurt for the sour cream. It will turn watery and you'll wonder why you went to the trouble of making it in the first place."

("You'll be safe there," Oliver Saks' family told him the morning they shipped him off from war-time London to a boarding school in the countryside. His favorite aunt hugged him and handed him one of his favorite foods—a black radish. Even the vegetable's appearance suggests dankness and deprivation—rough, lumpy, pitch-black. Standing on a drizzly train platform, the boy who became a world-famous neurologist held what looked like a damp lump of coal.)

While Sophie watched, I lined up three ugly black radishes—the full-blast, sour cream, olive oil, a lemon wedge, salt, and black pepper. Then she had me peel and finely grate the radishes, add four or five tablespoons of sour cream, "More if you like," three teaspoons of olive oil, a squeeze of lemon. Salt and freshly ground pepper. "Let it stand. The mixture can become very strong, which can be remedied by adding more sour cream." Later she spread it on thin buttered slices of dark bread.

THAT AUGUST, IMMIGRANT BOYS torched cars in the Paris suburbs and set upon the police with flare guns and ax handles. The government was slow to respond. There was talk of "zero tolerance." In August, most of Paris is empty.

Tourists flood into the city's center. Every Parisian who's able leaves for a house in the country or on the coast, or to relax in Spain, Florida, or Morocco. Those who don't leave move through an abandoned city. On August 15, the Feast of the Assumption, few businesses open. It's difficult to buy bread, even harder to get a dinner invitation.

During the empty Paris August I met the Morand family— friends of friends who'd been told I was alone and at loose ends. Two of the three Morand children had apartments in the city. The parents kept a home in the country, ninety minutes away. Lucie, the eldest Morand daughter, called and invited me to spend the weekend at her parents' country home. I stared at the late northern twilight. I said I'd be glad to go.

Our train passed through gray neighborhoods on the city's periphery. Soviet-style apartment blocks loomed over narrow dismal streets. Young immigrant toughs swaggered through those streets carrying live little monkeys on their shoulders, pirate-style.

The Morands' garden was large. Lucie's father had built walkways that meandered through grape arbors and between espaliered pears. He'd also built a small gravel patio, surrounded by box hedges, where we sometimes ate. Our lunches and dinners began with *pâté de foie gras*, goose liver *pâté*. Later, in the winter, as my familiarity with the Morands deepened, and whole goose livers were available in markets,

Madame Morand would poach one or two and serve us thick musky slices with rounds of toast.

Many years before, on a Bordeaux farm, I'd watched a farmer fatten a goose. With a cigarette dangling from his lips, the farmer marched in muddy black galoshes toward his honking victim. With one hand he grabbed the bird's neck, with the other he forced open its yellow beak. He inserted a long-necked plastic funnel down the squirming bird's throat and into it poured a quantity of milk and ground corn. This massive meal, repeated three times a day for several months, resulted in *foie gras*, fat liver. I didn't then know that alcoholism and diabetes produced a similar condition in humans called hepatic lipidosis. I knew only that *foie gras*, rich as butter, tasted good. I didn't let my pleasure be spoiled by another's misfortune.

On late Friday afternoons Lucie and I, and sometimes her younger sister Hélène, took the train to the Morand family home. Hervé, their brother, whom Lucie called a genius, lived in Belgium and only rarely came to Paris. Hélène said Hervé didn't get along with their parents.

French families aren't the cold closed units you may have heard they are. They're open to outsiders, especially Americans, who provide an impressionable audience for family dramas and offer new and interesting opportunities for gossip. The Morands took me to their hearts because, I think, I liked to eat. They did, too, perhaps more than most Frenchmen. I was told that one Christmas, the genius Hervé had in defiance of his parents gotten drunk and eaten an entire goose liver. He stood naked in the icy backyard and yelled that he was going to fail his high school finals on purpose. Hervé, Lucie confided to me, was always "very passionate."

I had a hard time putting my finger on the Morands' particular unhappiness. The father, a successful lawyer, was always happy to treat me to good wine and cognac. The mother knitted me a navy-blue wool sweater. But once while returning to Paris, Lucie told me that Hélène had, in her early twenties, tried several times to kill herself. Hervé didn't seem to do much in Brussels other than drink and write plays that were never produced. He never married. He never dated. Once during dinner Lucie's mother grabbed her by the wrists and asked me and several other guests, "Doesn't Lucie have an old maid's hands?"

Lucie's mother kept house. In her free time she knitted, or she painted ceramics. While she knitted or painted she listened to obscure radio stations that complained about youngsters' bad French grammar and insinuated that maybe the far right had a few good points. Lucie's mother didn't like Paris. "It hasn't been the same," she said, "since the war."

I met Hervé only once when he came down from Brussels for Easter. At Sunday lunch, there was some tension around the *foie gras*. Monsieur Morand alluded to Hervé's incident and Hervé stormed off to the living room where he drank and several times watched a video of Polanski's *Repulsion*. Lucie stood in the doorway and in a sweet voice begged him to please come back to the table. Hélène toyed with her food and looked miserable.

I don't remember how or why I lost touch with them. Whenever I ate *foie gras* I thought of them. I kept tabs through a mutual friend. Lucie married a doctor and had a baby. Hélène married and divorced twice. Then one January a mutual friend called to say Hervé had slit his wrists in Brussels. Lucie, the friend said, was "destroyed." I wondered aloud about the Morand family sadness.

"You know," the friend said, "that family has always had difficulties."

But what, I wondered, could they have been?

"Lucie adored Hervé. It was obvious to anyone who wasn't blind. If you didn't know you should at least have guessed that while teenagers, Lucie and Hervé were lovers."

EUROPEANS, PARTICULARLY THE French, say they better appreciate the taste of time—aged cheese, aged wine, moldy *pâtés*, game left to hang till almost putrescent. But our New World food has been handed down to us by history's dirty hands. The shiny avocado fruit is ancient.

As early as 6000 B.C. it was cultivated in the Tehuacan Valley of Mexico. Despite avocado's similarity to *avogado*,

Spanish for "attorney," the word avocado comes from *ahua-catl*, the Aztec for "testicle." When you sit watching the Super Bowl, the guacamole you eat with tortilla chips is identical to *ahuaca mulli*, an avocado sauce prepared by the Aztecs.

They loved turkey, too, and duck, tomatoes, and floppy-jowled plump hairless dogs. The greatest warriors and wealth-iest merchants sometimes paid to have a slave sacrificed at the temple. After his still-beating heart was offered to the gods, the unfortunate body was tossed down the temple's many steps. The body tumbled down to priests waiting to hack it to pieces. They distributed small portions of the flesh among the warrior's, or merchant's, family and friends, who used it to make human stew. Nothing elaborate, really. Just water, corn, a pinch of salt.

Squeamish moderns who fret over veal and worry that foot-ball brutalizes society, have difficulty imagining their way back to the Aztec kitchen. We know that every culture devel-ops its own particular intelligence for cooking, and that likes and dislikes change over centuries. We don't often appreciate that we share pleasures, like guacamole.

Every once in a while, apparently, an Aztec priest would skin a human sacrifice. He'd use the skin as a dance costume. To the Aztec layperson, this was business as usual. The same palates that had savored human stew also enjoyed avocado. They knew that, when toasted, its leaves had a spicy-sweet taste, a flavor they incorporated into mole. As for the green smooth flesh, it needed something acid, like lime, or tomato, to cut its richness, and maybe some chopped . . . onion, and minced coriander to pep it up. Hundreds of years later, our mouths understand this combination. (The conquering Spaniards grew fond of *ahuaca mulli*, and also liked avocado sprinkled with sugar.)

Spanish brutality displaced Aztec brutality, foreign corruption supplanted the indigenous. Eventually even the Spaniards disappeared, intermarrying into what was left of the Aztec population. Tremendous churches were built where the temples once stood. No one remembered anymore what human stew tasted like. Now on Super Bowl Sunday we go to the supermarket and buy a few high-priced Mexican avocados and tortilla chips. The crowd on the television roars. Bullish men charge each other. We set the guacamole on the coffee table and a few minutes later it's gone.

chapter five

*F*LEUR DU MAQUIS, a sheep's milk cheese from Corsica, looks like something an animal buried in a forest. Squat, round, semi-soft, it is covered with hairy gray mold and what appears to be dirt and bits of twig. *Fleur du maquis* looks like something only a brave person might poke at with a stick.

Its name means "flower of the underbrush," *maquis* meaning, in French, "underbrush." *Prendre le maquis*, "to take to the underbrush," is how the French say "to go underground" —the Maquis was the French underground organization that resisted the German Occupation. The *maquis* in the cheese's name refers not to the famous, if ineffectual, French Resistance, but to the scrub which covers much of Corsica. The debris coating *fleur du maquis* is composed of crushed rosemary, powdered thyme, savory, juniper berries—things which make up the Corsican *maquis*.

Napoleon was Corsican and after the Battle of Marengo in 1800, he wrote to Josephine, "*Ne te lave pas. Je reviens.*" Don't bathe. I'm coming home.

Two weeks passed before Napoleon returned to Paris. The Battle of Marengo took place in mid-June, a warm and humid time in the French capital: Napoleon was asking Josephine to literally stew in her own juices. The French like their women, and their cheeses, to be ripe. (Even today, of all Europeans, the French use the least soap, and bathe the least often.)

"The scent of her underarms easily uncaged the animal in men," is how French novelist Joris-Karl Huysmans described one of his heroines. The secret of this woman's animal-liberating armpits was a bacterial process not unlike that in ripening cheese. What aroused Napoleon and Huysmans, and what arouses any lover of strong cheese, is the odor of fermentation. (*Fleur du maquis* is also known as "Brin d'Amour," Morsel of Love.)

As a cheese like *fleur du maquis* ages, micro-organisms release protein-breaking enzymes that cause the cheese to become soft and, eventually, runny. Chemical by-products of this breakdown give ripe cheese its odor and flavor. Many different kinds of micro-organisms are used in cheese making, and each does its job a little differently. A mold related to penicillin, *Penicillum candidum*, gives Camembert its characteristic texture and flavor; a bacterium, *Brevibacterium linens* does the same for Limburger.

Much of the flavor in a young *fleur du maquis* comes from its herby crust. Only later, when its bone-white interior becomes runny, does the cheese have a high odor, slightly ammoniac, but not unpleasant. Even at its ripest, however, *fleur du maquis* can't compare to Alsatian Munster which, at its ripest, when its russet crust cracks to reveal a semi-liquid interior, smells like a barnyard on a hot summer day.

This barnyardy smell comes, in part, from ammonia produced by bacterial action. Ammonia is present in animal and human waste, and was originally distilled from camel dung many centuries ago at the Temple of Jupiter Ammon in Libya. Our noses are particularly sensitive to ammonia and other by-products of bacterial decomposition, like those responsible for underarm odor. Jacobson's Organ—two tiny pits on either side of the nasal septum, a centimeter and a half above the human nostril—specifically senses the smells beloved by Napoleon and routes the information to the most primal parts of the brain.

The odor of ripe cheese is so overpowering because it triggers, at the deepest level, all our associations of fecundity and decay, of sex and death. (French anthropologist Claude Lévi-Strauss wrote of American troops in Normandy who, during the war, incinerated a caveful of ripening Roquefort because they mistook the smell for that of rotting corpses.) To be fair, not all Frenchmen are comfortable with strong cheese. But one Parisian girl I knew waited until the end of the week to visit the Marché d'Aligre, not far from the Bastille, when the cheese-vendors' wares were the ripest. She always bought several small wheels of Alsatian Munster and, on her shopping days, if you were waiting for her in her apartment and the wind was right, you could smell her coming up the dark winding staircase. She'd serve the cheese at the end of her weekend dinner parties. As if the Munster didn't already have enough flavor, she presented the gooey wheels with a small bowl of cumin seeds. Her more delicate guests reeled backward from the dinner table, napkins clamped over their noses, eyes bulging—"My God!" "What is that stench?" She didn't mind. She'd smear a glob of Munster on a piece of baguette, sprinkle it with cumin seeds, and smile. "*Qu'est-ce que c'est bon!*" "It's sooo good." She was a sensualist and, I think, something of a sadist.

It took me a while to figure out that she was adept at juggling four, perhaps more, boyfriends at one time. On a drizzly February afternoon, in the dim light of her heavily curtained bedroom, I discovered a plastic sack containing a number of men's undershirts, all unlaundered. When I confronted her with them she reacted with complete calm, as if keeping a collection of dirty undershirts were the most normal thing in the world. Picking them one by one from the sack, she said, "That one is Fabrice, that one is Jean-François," and so on. She did not, I noticed, have one of mine.

FRIED BUTTER

I ATE TWO NIGHTS every week at a café on the Rue de Charonne. A small middle-class place with tables too close, and white paper napkins. The plastic menus were sticky. The old-fashioned bar was made of real zinc. If you sat at one of the café's lace-curtained windows, you had a view of the street, the life of the street, which in the early evening was a view of men and women, office workers mostly, making their way home from the Charonne metro station, one block away.

I went to this café because it bought its bread from a nearby bakery, one of few left in Paris that made good bread. The bakery had a trapdoor in the floor, just behind the register, from which the baker emerged like a floury jack-in-the-box, baguettes in the crook of his hairy arm. I also went to this café because it served good couscous. The cook worked in a closet-size kitchen. On his breaks he sat at one of the small tables, smoked, sipped coffee, and talked with the café's owner and with Djamal, the owner's nephew, who worked the bar and waited tables. These men were Kabyles, a Berber-speaking minority from Algeria. They liked me and they were kind to me and with them I felt at home.

Djamal was a proud Kabyle. "We are oppressed in Algeria," he said. "We are second-class citizens." He said that half of the 500,000 Algerians in France were Kabyles. He told me that couscous was a Berber, not an Arabic, word. He told me how the cook made couscous by rubbing dampened semolina flour against the side of a bowl. When steamed, these handmade granules, unlike machine-made couscous, were lighter and, said Djamal, "easier to digest."

I would start my meal with Bibb lettuce in a vinaigrette that I sopped with crusts of the café's good bread. Djamal made a little ceremony of setting before me a platter of raisin-studded couscous, and beside it a bowl of mutton, chickpeas, onions, and turnips, all swimming in clear pungent broth. On my plate I built a fluffy mound of couscous, ladled over it the broth, meat, and vegetables. Satisfied with my construction, I wagged a finger in the air and asked Djamal for a pitcher of rosé. He and his uncle politely watched me eat.

One slow evening Djamal lingered at my table. He asked if I was enjoying my couscous. In the same casual tone he asked if I was a Jew.

"I don't mean to be indiscreet," he said. "But in France, we all have to stick together." The French didn't distinguish between Algerian Kabyle and Algerian Arab, or between Arabs, Kabyles, and Jews. *"Ici, nous sommes tous des étrangers."* Here we are all foreigners.

The woman who ran the corner laundry was Serb. The green grocer across the street was Moroccan. An East Indian family from Mauritius owned the neighborhood hardware store. In my building's foyer on the evening before Rosh Hashanah a neighbor whispered to me, *"Shanah tovah."* Happy New Year, in Hebrew. I must have looked surprised.

"My wife thought you were a Jew," he said. "I wasn't sure.

If you don't have a place to go tomorrow night, you're welcome to eat with us."

Five minutes from my whispering neighbor stood Place Léon Blum, named after the premier whose one-year tenure in 1936 aroused hatred in France. A bit further was the Marais, the "swamp," the city's ancient Jewish quarter. Of the 50,000 Jews who lived there before the war, one tenth survived. At the very tip of Ile de la Cité, a tiny island in the Seine not far from the Marais, was a monument to the deported. I never went to see it.

One cold night when exiting Charonne Station I saw a mound of flowers before a plaque I'd never noticed. The plaque commemorated the death of nine people who, in February, 1962, were killed during a demonstration against the Algerian War. The police had charged a crowd of protestors who then tried to escape into the station. The dead were either trampled in the rush, or they were beaten by the police. It wasn't clear. It wasn't clear because at the time the Paris prefecture of police was Maurice Papon, a man who during the war had signed the warrants that sent 1,560 French Jews to Auschwitz.

Papon had an unusual career. On the night of October 17, 1961, he dispatched ten thousand police to central Paris to disperse Algerians demonstrating for Algeria's independence.

"The police did what they had to do," Papon said at the time.

What the police did at the time was kill two hundred men and women, crushing the heads of some with paving stones, shooting others at point-blank range. The police dumped bodies into the Seine where they floated downstream to Rouen.

When I look at a map of Paris, I see clearly where I once lived. I see the narrow cul-de-sac where my apartment was and, not far away, Place Léon Blum. Beyond it, the Marais. With my finger I trace the Rue de Charonne. I can picture Djamal's cafe. When I visited several years ago not much had changed. Djamal's uncle and the cook were idly chatting. Djamal was nowhere to be seen.

"He's gone to Chicago on a scholarship," his uncle told me. "He wants to be an engineer. He left just like that, with no warning. He was like a son to me."

chapter six

THEY'RE AN ODD LOCAL pair. One is dark black and six feet tall. Dreadlocks fall to his waist. The other is younger, Cambodian, short. He has no left eye. The flesh on that side of his face looks as though it had melted and been reformed by clumsy thumbs.

Every morning at around seven o'clock the black man pushes his shopping cart out of the alley across the street. He whistles. A minute or so later the Cambodian boy, from around the corner, whistles back. He appears, smiling. "Frank, oh, Frank. My friend," he says. The two begin their day.

They have a circuit, a routine. They start with the alley behind my house. While I sip my coffee and read the *Los Angeles Times*, I hear them. Frank grunts and hoists the boy into Dumpsters where he searches for aluminum cans, glass and plastic bottles.

"Sing for me, Frank," the boy says from deep in the Dumpster.

"OK, Little Man." Frank clears his throat, spits. In his clear tenor he sings, "Precious Lord." Little Man tosses cans and bottles out of the Dumpster. One after another they clatter to the ground. Frank gathers them up, again clears his throat, sings "Proud Mary." With a wire hanger, he taps the rhythm on the Dumpster while Little Man forages. "Rollin', row-ho-lin' on the riv-uh." Tap-tap-tap.

By around eleven they've lashed several black bags filled with bottles and cans to Frank's shopping cart. They go to a recycling center eight blocks away. They come back and buy a big bottle of beer from the small corner store near my house. They sit in the shade of a garage at the end of my alley. They drink. Dizzy, flushed, Little Man grows animated. He tells Frank about a girl he saw who had big tits. Frank takes a long draw from the bottle of beer. "Shit," he says, "all you talk is shit. You never had no pussy." He passes the bottle to Little Man who with his good eye squints at the sun and says, "Someday." He drinks, he coughs. Beer sprays out his nose.

"Don't go wastin' that shit," says Frank, reaching for the bottle.

In my neighborhood's natural ecology, Little Man and Frank never go dry. Many Mexican immigrants also live here. Most work as day laborers in construction. On late weekday afternoons they line up at the corner store and buy cases of beer. They don't care about recycling. They toss their empties into the Dumpsters behind the crowded apartments where they live. Frank and Little Man sell the empties to buy more beer.

Sundays are the wettest. The Mexican men rise early and go to Mass. Afterward, in white shirts, blue jeans, and polished boots, they stand beside their pickup trucks parked before their apartments, radios blaring love songs. They drink beer after beer. They stagger to the corner store for more. I mention in passing to my neighbor, a Mexican woman, that I feel bad for the men, so far from their wives and kids. She laughs. She tells me, "Where I'm from in Mexico, on Sunday afternoons I've seen the same sort of men passed out drunk in the town square. All they care about is drinking beer on Sundays with their friends. Their wives and kids sit at home. The men. It's always men, isn't it?"

On Mondays, or any day after a big televised basketball, football, or soccer game, Frank and Little Man stay busy. They make many trips to the corner store. I see them supine beside the garage in the alley. They chat dreamily. Little Man waves his hands while he talks. He turns on his side to face Frank, who mutters, chuckles, burps. With a finger Little Man brushes something—dirt? a blade of grass?—from the tip of Frank's nose.

Frank, I know, sleeps behind an oleander hedge in the

backyard of an ancient woman who keeps a dozen cats. Little Man belongs to an extended family that occupies two houses several blocks away. I sometimes see Little Man's father, a batik sarong cinched at his waist, on his way to buy menthol cigarettes at the corner store. Four or five little girls swarm around his knees. At the store they tug his sarong and beg him in English to buy chewing gum.

A while back, in the middle of a week when there had been no big games on TV, I saw Frank and Little Man meet on the corner across from my house. The morning was warm. Sunlight shone on Frank's sweaty forehead. As Little Man approached, Frank held a big bottle of beer in the air, like an athlete waving a trophy. Little Man ran to him. He laughed. He was so happy he reached out to take Frank's free hand. Frank pulled away. "Don't," he said. "Don't try that faggot shit on me."

MY FRIEND REZA WAS calling from Los Angeles to talk about the results of the Iranian election. He was excited that the reformers had done so well, but a few minutes later his enthusiasm dissolved into melancholy. The elections were an excuse for him to talk about exile.

"When I was little and walking home from school I would turn down this alley onto our street. It was a very narrow street in a typical middle-class neighborhood in central Teheran. Mostly two-story houses, white, beige, gray. Some families decorated the front of their houses with little ceramic tiles. And when I turned onto our street you could hear the sounds of dishes clattering, people talking, someone arguing. The sounds of our neighbors. And everyone's kitchen window looked out on the street. And when I turned onto our street, if I smelled saffron coming from our kitchen, I knew someone special was coming for dinner—an uncle, an aunt, someone nice.

"The reason I could smell the saffron was that if you ever cooked anything very nice, very special, you always opened your kitchen window so your neighbors could smell it. If it was something that smelled very, very good, you had to take your neighbors a plate of it. Saffron was a way of showboating, of showing-off. It meant that you were well-to-do, or you had company coming. In Iran, you always give guests the best of everything. The best bed. The best blanket. The best food. And because saffron was something expensive, you used it when you cooked for guests. Rich people ate saffron with their rice all the time, but in our middle-class neighborhood, it was something that you ate maybe only once a week.

"So to me, whenever I smell it, I remember this feeling of excitement I got when I was coming home from school. Now, it reminds me of Iran. Iranians think Iran produces the best saffron in the world, even better than Spain. Persians have used saffron forever. It's always been a special thing. The Moguls who invaded Iran took saffron with them when they invaded

India, and that's how the Indians started to use it. My mother used to toast the threads of saffron and then grind them in a mortar and pestle with just a pinch of sugar. She would mix the saffron with butter and then pour it onto rice. She loved the color, and when guests came, God bless her, she always liked to have at least three different colors of rice. She would color it with spinach, or with spices. Three colors of rice and two different colors of stew. And she sent a plate to our neighbors—our neighbors in the back, and our neighbors to the right.

"The custom was that when they returned the empty plate, they always put a flower on it, usually a rose. Everybody had a small garden and there were always roses in it. Whenever our neighbors brought us food, my mother always sent me to the garden fast, like it was an emergency. 'Go and pick a rose!' It couldn't wait.

"When I first came to Los Angeles, one day my wife made some bread. It's called *ghata* in Persian, and it's made with eggs and butter and sugar. It smelled wonderful when it was baking, and so, to be nice, I took some to our neighbors across the hall. They seemed really surprised. The next day they just left the empty plate in front of our door. They didn't knock. They didn't say thank you. They just left the plate there. I couldn't believe it.

"I guess I should have understood that I was new to this country and I shouldn't have expected anything. But this made me angry and when I saw the neighbor, the husband, in the parking lot the next day, I said, 'You know, what you did really showed that you don't have much class.' And he said, 'What do you mean?' And I told him about the plate and he said, 'Well, we just left it there because we didn't want to disturb you.'

"That was my first lesson in being neighbors in America. It left a very bad taste in my mouth. Maybe it was just that guy, that family. Maybe they were jerks. At the hospital where I work, I've been called a 'camel jockey' a few times, and it's ridiculous because in Iran we don't even have camels. Now, I don't even know who my neighbors are. We never talk. And there are times when I'm cooking something nice, something good, and I'm using saffron, and in the back of my head I have this response, this instinct, and I think, 'Maybe I should take some to my neighbors.' But I don't. I don't know how they'll react. I don't know if they'll like the food. Now saffron is something just for my guests and family."

chapter seven

THE MORNING OF THE recent fire I left my
kitchen window open. Oblivious to all but my own
troubles, it wasn't until I stood on my front porch,
staring at the yellowish dawn, watching what looked like
snow flutter down on my front lawn, that I realized the
mountains to the east were burning. I sipped my coffee, felt
something odd on my tongue. Ashes from ten thousand acres
of sage and mesquite, burning thirty miles away, had found
their way into my cup.

The last time I'd eaten ashes was years ago in Jerusalem, as part of my meal before Tisha B'Av, the ninth day of the month of Av, which falls in midsummer. The First Temple and Second Temple were destroyed on Tisha B'Av. In the Bar Kochba revolt against the Romans, the last Jewish fortress also fell on that day in 135 A.D. Exactly one year later, the land where the Second Temple had once stood was plowed under. In 1492, Spain's King Ferdinand chose Tisha B'Av as the last day Jews would be allowed on Spanish soil. On Tisha B'Av the First World War began, the necessary prelude to the Second. On Tisha B'Av, from sundown to sundown, you afflict yourself by not eating, drinking, or bathing. You sit on low stools or on the floor. The very pious sleep with a stone for a pillow. The evening before, you eat a boiled egg dipped in ashes. You go to synagogue where by candlelight you read the Book of Lamentations.

A French cheese called *morbier* has a thin line of tasteless ash down its middle. The ash supposedly separates the morning milk from the evening milk and is one of the few instances I know where the eating of ashes is benign. I remember a study of people with unusual eating disorders published in *The New England Journal of Medicine*. One gentleman, who compulsively licked ashtrays clean, was found to have an iron deficiency. About the same time the study was published I remember reading about a fellow named Carlos in Chico, California. Police arrested Carlos for having stolen and eaten the cremated remains of four people. While he might have had an iron deficiency, Carlos said he hoped his diet of cremains would bring him "everlasting life." (Brazil's Yanomomi Indians burn their dead and eat the ashes with banana paste.)

Ashes fill the Hebrew Bible. Time and again people are warned that if they misbehave, they'll end up wallowing in ashes, a sign of repentance. In the Psalms, King David writes that his days are "consumed like smoke." Maybe he was mourning Absalom, his wayward son. King David writes that in his sorrow he has eaten ashes "like bread." Covered with boils from the soles of his feet to the crown of his head, poor Job sits himself down in ashes. His wife's advice: "Curse God and die."

The mountain fire is out. A thin film of ash coats the miniature greenhouse beside the garage. The brilliant sunsets will be no more. I find ashes in a bowl of apples I keep by the kitchen window. I drag a finger through the white powder and taste it. Although it could be the remains of incinerated squirrel or lizard, the powder tastes of nothing.

"I weep. Mine eye, mine eye runneth down with water because the comforter that should relieve my soul is far from me."

We read those words as we knelt on the cold stone floor in the study hall of the yeshiva I attended. The candles we held flickered. Around me, young men wept aloud for Jerusalem's long-ago desolation. I was younger then, and secure in faith, and could realize with clarity sorrow other than my own.

SOMEWHERE, PERHAPS IN GREGOR Von Rezzori's *Memoirs of an Anti-Semite*, I remember reading of Bucharest Jews eating raw garlic. My father, a Transylvanian, always did. At every dinner he ate three or four raw cloves which, with great delicacy, he peeled and sliced very thin. With his knife he balanced a slice of garlic atop each forkful of pot roast or baked chicken or lamb chop that he aimed toward his mouth. "Heaven," he'd smack his lips and sigh. He'd squeeze my mother's thigh and make her jump. "Heaven, babe."

Garlic was not always as American as it is now. In 1971, Alice Waters began serving baked heads of garlic and hot fresh loaves of bread as an appetizer at Chez Panisse in Berkeley, California. Back then, such a simple thing was regarded as a culinary revelation.

Berkeley. The Free Speech Movement. The Black Panthers. Cesar Chavez. Alcatraz. The Six Day War. The sudden and militant valorization of ethnicity. It took what amounted to a revolution to launch garlic toward respectability in the middle-American kitchen. Prejudices against garlic go deep. The Hindu caste system, an ancient distillation of Aryan sensibility, forbids garlic to the three highest castes—Brahmans, Kshatriyas, Vaisyas. Hindu religious texts categorize garlic as *rajasic*, or a "food in the mode of passion," and passion, presumably, is something the highest castes, and those seeking spiritual enlightenment, should avoid. (In Iran, another Aryan outpost, garlic's use is relatively rare and light.) In ancient Greece, garlic was fit for soldiers, laborers, and oarsmen, but the upper classes were repulsed by its smell. In America, garlic was long considered low class, associated with hot-blooded foreigners, passionate and licentious people like the French, Italians, and Jews. (In Numbers 11:5 the Israelites pine for the garlic they ate while slaves in Egypt.)

Garlic-fearing elites perhaps had a point. Biochemists have recently discovered that certain chemicals in garlic stimulate the production of nitric oxide synthase, an enzyme primarily responsible for erectile function in men. Heightened male libido portends anarchy: uncertain paternity, confused inheritance rights, racial pollution, blurred class boundaries. The high-minded could make a case that in America garlic's popularity has mapped snugly with sexual freedom. The first Gilroy Garlic Festival was held in 1978. One year later disco diva Donna Summer moaned her way through "Love to Love You Baby."

I would instead make the case that garlic made my parents' marriage a long and happy one. In the late 1960s and early 1970s many of my playmates' parents—non-garlic-eaters— filed for divorce. My parents remained in love. The image of the two of them alone, apart, stays with me. Because I was born and raised in Southern California, these are subtropical memories—my mother in a loose shift dress, my father in shirtsleeves, the two of them walking somewhat ahead of me, speaking in low voices, laughing.

There are other reasons, I think, that garlic is so intimate. When you chop, mince, or crush garlic with your hands, the smell is difficult to remove. Garlic breath lingers for hours. Garlic marks you in the way certain animals mark trees or nests with their musk glands. The analogy isn't far off: garlic's odor-producing chemicals contain sulfur compounds similar to ones found in animal musk and, frankly, in digestive gas and waste. These compounds, called mercaptins, are also present in the durian, an infamous Asian fruit whose creamy, sweet flesh smells like sewage. In light of garlic's reputation, durian eating is believed, not surprisingly, to arouse sexual desire. The Javanese say, "When the durians come down, sarongs are soon to follow."

I remember an aura of garlic radiating from my father's dinner plate. He was served first—the best slice of roast, the chicken breast, the biggest lamb chop, were his. Once served, he began his garlic ritual, and the smell of it would drift across the table toward me. "What else can I get you?" my mother would ask him, her hand on his shoulder. On her way to and from the kitchen she'd stop to kiss the top of his head. During an especially good meal, he'd plant a greasy kiss on her cheek. "You've outdone yourself, babe." "Your mustache," she'd laugh, "tickles."

My father is now cold and dead and he, like all the dead, seems resolute in staying so. Not long ago he appeared to my mother in a dream that disturbed her. "He wasn't the handsome man I remember. I could see every line, every wrinkle, every age spot on his face. His complexion was horrible," she told me. "Of course, Ma," I said. "He's dead. You can't look any worse than that."

He doesn't visit me in dreams, but the smell of garlic on my fingers reminds me of him and, by extension, the loss of him. Sulfurous, maybe a little shameful, the smell reminds me of love.

chapter eight

RAIN FALLS. THIS TIME of year, says my almanac, it ought not. The air smells of wet asphalt and dirt. The afternoon light looks dingy. A cabbage white, *Pieris rapae*, surprising in the dingy light, flits across my backyard. The butterfly makes dizzy arcs to my beloved garden where rain-heavy arugula bends to the ground.

A breeze staggers the cabbage white. Its flouncy wings camouflage ruthlessness. The cabbage white descends on my patch of arugula. Curling its body into an inverted comma, it deposits a tiny rocket-shaped egg on each leaf. I feel a pang. In seven days, the eggs will hatch. Velvety green caterpillars will start to eat. They'll feast till my arugula is gone, again.

The cabbage white's nature is to munch and ruin. What it's after is cruciferae, the vegetable family to which cabbage, and arugula, belong. Cruciferae contain mustard oil. After devouring cruciferae, cabbage white larva are unpalatable to predators. Cabbage whites are hard to beat. Every year I've tried to grow arugula, cabbage whites appear. I'm dumbstruck by their tenacity. I could use insecticides, I suppose, but they've never helped much.

It's the cabbage white's nature to eat, and mine to grow arugula. I grow it because of a blonde I knew, a beautiful girl with literary ambitions. She was given to depression. Her skin and hair had a pleasant, vaguely chlorinated smell. Her eyes also suggested water. You've seen the color in Hawaiian postcards: the clear shallows where islands once were. She liked to swim. In the summer she'd sneak into better hotels and lounge beside their pools.

Afterward she'd call and suggest we have dinner.

"Buy me lamb chops," she'd say. "Lamb chops. And arugula for salad. I love arugula."

Her apartment had a large white-enameled stove. While she waited for me, she preheated the broiler. She'd greet me at the door, sweat beading her nose and neck. She held a gin martini in one hand. Vodka, she said, made her sweat. Behind her, in the hot dark apartment, a record played on the stereo. Maybe Mama Cass singing "Dream a Little Dream of Me."

I washed the arugula while she watched. Then I put it in a pillow case and took it outside and spun it over my head. I dressed the arugula with olive oil and lemon juice, and sometimes with crumbled blue cheese. I lovingly rubbed the lamb chops with garlic. While they broiled, the blonde and I danced. Then we'd eat with abandon, mostly.

At dinner's end, she'd drag her long fingers through the olive oil at the bottom of the salad bowl. She'd lick her fingers clean. And some nights, later on, with her hand on my chest, she'd talk in a hushed voice about money. She needed money. She was, she knew, bad with money. The landlord was pestering her. So was the phone company. She smelled of lamb, garlic, and mustardy arugula.

Time passed. Her invitations to dinner grew few. We'd still meet around town for drinks. One time I met her and she was with a man, a Brazilian attorney with slicked-back hair. She seemed happy.

Some weeks later she called late at night. She'd argued with the Brazilian.

"All I did was ask him for a loan. I can't believe someone so rich could be so tight. Maybe it's a Brazilian thing. A Third World thing. You know, an exaggerated fear of scarcity. I don't know. Anyway, he's gone."

I heard her light a cigarette, exhale.

"I just made a shaker of martinis. Ice cold. Want to come over for a drink?"

The fancy grocery store I sometimes go to sells prewashed

arugula in plastic bags. When I buy it, I feel defeated. With enough attention, arugula should be easy to grow. Maybe this year I'll be lucky. A while back I saw the blonde in the gourmet shop. She was at the butcher counter buying a rack of lamb. I wanted to hide, but our eyes met. She was thinner. Her face was unlined. She'd married, she said. An architect. She'd become "quite domestic." She hefted the rack of lamb in her palms. She had to rush. She was making dinner, for friends.

JUAN SLEEPS ON MY couch. I've known him since I was a young man. Our lives took different directions. Last night he knocked at my door. "I'm sorry to bother you. I need to stay with you tonight."

The day before, he explained, he had waited in line for five hours to cross the border.

"The immigration officers have to type everyone's name into a computer. But they don't know how to type. It takes them forever. They're afraid of terrorists coming into America. The Arabs are making me suffer."

He says he's tired and hungry. I ask him if he's ever eaten Thai food. He says no. I tell him I was just about to make dinner, a spicy beef salad called *laab*. The ingredients sit in my refrigerator.

I make us a drink of tequila, tomato juice, lime juice, and

cumin. We drink and talk about everything but September 11. Juan comes from a family of ten children that migrated to Tijuana from Durango. He has three kids of his own. He works long hours in a San Diego restaurant kitchen. We don't see each other often. His family is so large, he always has stories to tell.

"My second youngest sister, Maria Jesús, isn't really my sister. She's my niece. My oldest brother's wife left him and Maria Jesús when Maria Jesús was a tiny baby. My parents took her and raised her as their daughter. Three months ago her mother appears in Tijuana. Just like that. Out of nowhere. She hasn't seen Maria Jesús for thirty years. She asks Maria Jesús to go with her back to Durango. And Maria Jesús goes. We haven't heard from her since."

He says it all in a deadpan way, then he laughs in the high falsetto Mexican men use when they laugh about absurdity. He and I start making *laab*. We sit at the kitchen table, chopping up lemon grass, onion, mint, cilantro, and small green chiles.

"I know all of these things," Juan says. "We have all of them in Mexico."

I show him my best Thai cookbook, Su-Mei Yu's *Cracking the Coconut*. He thumbs through it and points to a picture of sticky rice bundled in banana leaves. "We make something like that, too, in Mexico. A tamale wrapped in banana leaves."

What interests him most is how many of the recipes use chile. "Thai people," he says, "must be part Mexican."

The give and take is ancient. Chiles are indigenous to Central America. Portuguese traders introduced them to Asia in the early sixteenth century. (Cilantro, on the other hand, used in Mexican and Asian cuisines, is indigenous to the Mediterranean.) The result of this exchange is that you can go to any market in Mexico and, with few exceptions, find all the raw ingredients needed for making a decent Thai meal.

Juan asks to use the phone and calls his family in Tijuana. I mince sirloin, poach it, sprinkle it with fish sauce and lime. Juan is told his seventy-year-old mother has been hospitalized. She's having a hard time breathing. Juan's chin quivers. He says he's afraid to go back to Tijuana, that it's almost impossible to cross the border. He says he doesn't want to lose his job. He hangs up and stares at the phone.

I mix the beef with the herbs, onion, and chile. I scatter toasted rice powder on top. Juan takes second and third helpings. He asks for more chile. He says, "My mother would really like this salad. You should come to Tijuana and make it for her."

I wash dishes. Juan turns on the news: war and rumors of war. He pulls my atlas from the bookshelf. He studies the world map and with a finger traces a line from Afghanistan to New York to Tijuana. He flips the large pages to the map of Mexico. He chuckles when he finds the small town he's from in Durango.

He asks if he can stay with me for a while, until it's easier to get across the border. I tell him he's welcome to stay as long as he likes. He takes a shower, then settles on the couch. I go to bed. All night long I hear him get up and turn on the television. He watches the news. At around 3:00 a.m. the house is silent and Juan begins to snore.

TANGLED IN SWEATY SHEETS, I writhed in an overheated London hotel room. Outside, rain fell. Inside, the radiator hissed. The night before I'd eaten at a restaurant named Grumbles. Hours after my meal, the first waves of nausea hit. They raged until morning. Weak-kneed, clammy, I had a train to catch. I was going to visit my friend Leorah and her family.

Leorah and I had worked together for several years in Jerusalem. She was an intelligent, passionate girl. In the cause of Russian Jewry, she'd chained herself to several Soviet embassies. She'd often said, "If we're ever in England at the same time, you have to come visit my family in Manchester. It'll be fun."

Leorah's father greeted me at the door. Lush gray eyebrows shaded his eyes, giving him a keen, raptorial air.

"In case Leorah didn't tell you," he said, rubbing his palms together, "ours is a vegetarian household. We eat no meat of any kind. We hope you'll respect that."

He gazed at me as if he suspected I had a baron of beef hidden in my backpack. I suspected he was nuts.

The Talmud teaches that land has character, a personality bound up in its very soil. Land imparts its character to those who live and work upon it, which is why, for example, New Yorkers are different from Bostonians, Frenchmen from Italians. Since the early nineteenth century, Manchester has been a hotbed of ardent vegetarianism, has even been home to a number of "fructarians" who eat only windfallen fruit. (They're careful to spit out the seeds so as not to interfere with the life cycle of the plant.)

Like lead in old plumbing, Manchester had leached into Leorah and her family.

Her mother took my coat. "Let's feed you some lunch. How about a nice big bowl of my famous raw-fruit bran muesli?"

We sat around the kitchen table. In front of me sat a nice big bowl of the stuff Leorah's mother had whipped up in her food processor. Pineapple, carrots, apples, oranges, walnuts, and plenty of bran. (But no honey. "It's *stealing* from the bees," Leorah's father hissed.) Leorah, her mother, and father stared at me. The frothy, pulpy muesli was so rich in fiber that even a termite would have had a hard time digesting it.

"That's a boy," Leorah's father said. "Eat up. There's plenty more!"

Bran is essentially the husks of wheat that are removed when making flour. Bran contains a great deal of fiber. The entire point of fiber is that it is indigestible. It scours the intestines like steel wool. Had I, on all fours, grazed an entire meadow, I couldn't possibly have consumed more fiber than was contained in one bowl of Leorah's mother's muesli. The effect was immediate.

Cold sweat tingled on my forehead.

"Let's take a walk," Leorah said.

Bundled in coats and scarves, we wandered through hard Manchester rain. We wandered through working-class neighborhoods where wan children munched bags of greasy potato chips. The rain, always the rain. The muffled rumbling wasn't thunder, but bran muesli moving through my gut. We visited Leorah's old high school where I raced to the bathroom. I pressed my forehead against cool tile and silently prayed, "God, help me. Please help."

The walk back to Leorah's house was the longest in my life. We arrived in time for dinner. Vegetable soup. A salad of raw cauliflower and carrots. And many heavy thick slices of toasted bran bread. We retired to the overheated living room. My belly was distended, taut. I undid my belt. I leaned far back on the couch. Rain pelted the windowpanes. Leorah's father began to speak.

"I'll never forget the day I watched a lamb being led to slaughter. So docile. So innocent. So entirely unaware of what was about to happen."

Remembering how earlier in the day I'd innocently approached this gentleman's home, I sympathized with the lamb. Leorah's father waved his hands in the air. He called meat "corpse." He wanted to know why I ate corpse, why anyone would want to eat corpse. I looked to Leorah for rescue. I looked to her mother. They were both caught up in the father's evangelical hysteria. An enormous gas bubble, I could feel it, was making its way through my intestines. I was pale with pain. I leaned farther back on the couch. The bathroom, I knew, was only a few yards away. It might as well have been in Brazil. Leorah's father continued to rant about corpse. Disgusting, vile, repellent, nauseating corpse.

"And you eat the *violence*," he wailed. "When you eat corpse, you eat *fear* and *violence*!"

I certainly felt as though I'd eaten plenty fear and violence. If I didn't act fast, a lamb being led to slaughter would hardly remain the most frightful thing Leorah's father had ever seen. I stood and bounded to the bathroom, unzipping my pants as I ran. I didn't care. I slammed the door and experienced blissful, explosive relief.

The next morning Leorah's mother fed me another big bowl of raw-fruit bran muesli. I knew if I did not leave, I would surely die. I made some excuse to go back to London. Leorah and her parents hated to see me go. It was while I was on the train, chugging through more dense drizzle, each lurch of the car agitating my overstimulated gut, that I discovered that Leorah's mother had given me a farewell gift. When I wasn't looking, she'd tucked into my backpack a loaf of fresh bran bread. All the way back to the city, I thought of Jeffrey.

IN 1918, TWO YEARS after Margaret Sanger opened the nation's first birth-control clinic, Dr. Lulu Hunt Peters published *Diet & Health, with Key to Calories*, America's first diet book, which sold 800,000 hardback copies. During the Depression, Americans somehow lost interest in losing weight. The national obsession with dieting didn't revive until after World War II. (In 1961, the hardback edition of Julia Child's *Mastering the Art of French Cooking* sold only 650,000 copies.)

During those post-War years cottage cheese became a diet food, a "calorie smart" replacement for meat. The "diet plate" appeared on restaurant menus. A lump of white grainy curds parked on a lettuce leaf beside slices of canned cling peaches or mealy tomato. As America's hunger for thinness grew, so did its hunger for cottage cheese. Per capita consumption rose during the late '60s and reached its peak in 1972, when Americans were annually eating 5.4 pounds of the stuff.

Jeffrey, a distant cousin, discovered cottage cheese as a diet food in 1967. He was fourteen years old, five feet tall, 175 pounds, just as America was preparing for the Summer of Love.

Jeffrey wanted sex, which in 1967 wasn't an unusual aspiration for a fourteen-year-old boy. But Jeffrey was so uncomfortable with his plump body that he walked around in a ski parka. He was strolling down Madison Avenue in New York when he caught his reflection in a store window.

He said to himself, "It looks unusual to wear a ski parka in July. I better go home now."

Jeffrey's family lived in a nice apartment in the East 80s, not far from the Metropolitan Museum of Art. But between birth and thirteen years of age, Jeffrey was taken by his parents to spend each weekend with Sesha and Sasha, his maternal grandparents, who lived in a failed Communist commune near Mosholu Parkway in the Bronx.

"The commune," Jeffrey told me, "was named after Sholem Aleichem and was basically a complex of Tudor-style buildings built around a central courtyard. For some reason, in the hedge surrounding the complex, the commune's members had stuck dozens of red plastic roses."

Sesha, Jeffrey's Warsaw-born grandmother, had never mastered English. "Before" and "because," two such similar-sounding words, always confused her. "I had my breast removed because you were born," she'd tell Jeffrey. Or, "I was so happy before you were born."

Sesha fed Jeffrey as if he were a refugee child. Slices of rye bread heavily buttered on both sides. Cottage cheese smothered in sour cream. And, because she was an atheist, her *spécialité de la maison*, rare pork roast.

Whenever Sesha cooked lamp chops she made him eat the fat quickly, before it congealed. Jeffrey's weekends in Sesha's care made him plump. When he was thirteen, sprouting pubic hair, and in general becoming conscious of himself as a young man, he told his parents he would no longer return to the Bronx. Sesha took the news philosophically.

"Make sure he eats cottage cheese with lots of sour cream," she said, "because he becomes skinny."

Jeffrey's mother kept the family refrigerator well stocked with cottage cheese. On the afternoon Jeffrey realized that in the summer it was unusual to walk around the Upper East Side in a ski parka, he went home for a snack. Opening the refrigerator, he took out one of the many large containers of cottage cheese.

"There was a green film on top of the cheese," he said. "My mother was an artist and was always experimenting with Jell-O and food coloring to make our meals look more interesting. In our home, green cottage cheese wasn't much of a surprise. I just stirred it up and ate a spoonful. It tasted a little more sour than usual. I didn't think much of it. A few hours later I experienced violent intestinal evacuation."

After many trips to the bathroom, Jeffrey realized he'd hit upon something. He lost his appetite. He followed a strict diet. Every day he ate only a sandwich made from Pepperidge Farm bread and a slice of American cheese. For dessert, he ate a spoonful of the purgative green cottage cheese, which he hid at the back of the freezer.

"It worked," he said, "like magic."

Sitting became painful, and Jeffrey couldn't stray far from the toilet. He lay in his bedroom, listening to the radio and to the awful rumbling low in his gut. Outside, in the big world, hippies were said to hold orgies in Golden Gate Park. Jeffrey could imagine them chanting, "Make love, not war!"

He knew that down in the East Village, hordes of barefoot, middle-class kids crowded the sidewalks. They thronged the Free Store and the Psychedelicatessen. The Fugs performed at the Players Theater on Macdougal Street. Lethargic Jeffrey imagined himself down in the East Village, wandering barefoot in tropical heat. He imagined sweaty, long-haired girls, flimsy cotton clothes clinging to damp, braless bodies. He groaned and buried his head in his pillow and dozed off.

"By the end of August I'd lost forty pounds," he told me, mournfully, "I looked great. I didn't have a girlfriend. I'd slept through the Summer of Love."

chapter nine

BY THE MID-1970S, WHEN the Teamsters began making inroads into the United Farm Workers union, Lila, my doctor, felt she had been marching in demonstrations for too long. She felt frustrated. She was tired of *La Lucha*, The Struggle. So, twenty-five years ago she took a bus from Los Angeles to San Diego, and another bus from San Diego to Tijuana, and another from Tijuana, heading south to the state of Guerrero where, Lila hoped, she could lie on the beach, relax, and forget.

The red-and-white bus drove through deserts and forests, and down, slowly, to a barren, sea-level expanse called *El Infiernillo*, Little Hell, where the Mexican government had dammed the Rio Balsas and was building an enormous hydroelectric plant. Close to the coast, the bus passed through miles of coconut groves, and through a town called *El Naranjito*, Little Orange Tree, where, standing in front of a palm-thatched cantina, beautiful transvestites in shimmering dresses waited to entertain construction workers from the hydroelectric plant. The transvestites were more beautiful than the women of Guerrero.

Lila rented a hut near the beach from a man named Valentín. She dozed in a hammock. She swam. She ate papaya and spat the seeds onto the ground in front of her hut, where, in time, they began to sprout. Weeks passed. The same dry heat. The same blinding glare off the water. The same sound of the sea, day and night. Lila began to feel more hopeful and one morning she woke up, rolled out of her hammock and, reaching for her white tennis shoe, felt a searing pain in her little finger. It felt like someone had shoved a red hot needle through the skin, right through to the bone.

She looked in the shoe and saw a small brown scorpion staring back at her. Careful not to crush it completely, she thumped it with a magazine. Her palm was already numb when, a few minutes later, she showed the brown scorpion to Valentín.

"My God, baby," he said. "The nearest doctor's an hour away. Your only hope is to see Doña Toña."

Doña Toña, Lila recalls, was an ugly name and it belonged

to a medicine woman who lived in the sandy hills, a thirty-minute hike from the beach. Lila had no choice. The numbness had already spread above her wrist and was on its way, she knew, to her heart. Choking on white powdery sand, she followed Valentín up into the hills.

Doña Toña, a squat brown woman, was feeding chickens when Lila and Valentín arrived.

"Oh, my God," she said when Valentín showed her the scorpion. She looked at Lila, who was feeling light-headed. "Come inside."

Doña Toña's shack was made entirely of palm fronds. She'd filled it with candles and oil lamps. Bundles of herbs hung from the ceiling. Sooty statues of saints and photos of dead people crowded makeshift shelves. On a small table sat a bowl in which Doña Toña had stacked a perfect pyramid of yellow limes, what Americans call "Key limes," smaller and much more fragrant than the Persian variety grown in California. Lila could smell them from where she stood. In the dim shack, they seemed to glow. Doña Toña examined each fruit and chose one and cut it in half. With her finger she scooped out some pulp and studied it carefully. With a bit of old muslin she tied the halved lime to Lila's little finger. She dipped a boar's-hair brush into an oil lamp and painted a line around Lila's arm, just below her shoulder.

"The poison won't go past that line," Doña Toña said. "And whatever you do, don't let the lime fall off your finger."

"Are you sure this is going to work?" Lila asked.

Doña Toña looked at her as if she were deranged. "Of course."

Valentín guided Lila back down the hills and by the time they got to his house, the numbness had reached the line drawn in oil on Lila's arm. Valentín's wife helped her into a hammock. His five children came to stare. Lila was waving her hands in front of her face, grabbing at something invisible in the air before her nose.

"I'm growing a trunk," Lila told Valentín. "Like an elephant."

"*Una trompa? De elefante?*"

This was the most hilarious thing Valentín's children had ever heard. They cackled. "I'm an elephant, too! I'm an elephant, too!" They ran around the room, trumpeting like baby elephants. Valentín chased them outside. He tied the lime tighter to Lila's finger. Lila fell asleep.

For the rest of the day and all night long she tried to grab her phantom trunk. She could see it clearly—the wrinkly tough gray skin, the bristly hairs—but it evaded her grasp. She dreamt she was in Africa. She dreamt of elephants who seemed very proud of their trunks. They taunted her with displays of skill, ostentatiously using their trunks to pick tiny yellow limes from tall trees. No matter how hard Lila tried, she couldn't make her trunk work. She couldn't even touch it.

Late the following day she woke up. The lime was still tied to her finger, but her trunk had disappeared. Valentín's wife brought her fresh coconut milk, and in the afternoon Lila returned to her hut. The next morning the sun rose as it always does in that part of the world, dazzling and relentless. Lila felt fine.

Valentín took the scorpion to the transvestite cantina in *El Naranjito*. Impressed by Lila's story, the owner had the scorpion laminated into the bar counter. In Lila's honor he changed the cantina's name to The Elephant Bar, which, the transvestites complained, wasn't an elegant name at all.

LILA'S FRIEND ROSARIO never had a mind for politics. She was from a large and poor family that lived miserably in Mexicali, a city just across the Mexican border, one hundred and ten miles east of San Diego. By the time Rosario finished high school, two of her fourteen cousins had died of cirrhosis and the rest were aspiring to careers in petty thievery or drug peddling. Rosario wanted to be a doctor.

"I'm never coming back," Rosario told her mother the day she left to study at a San Diego university that had awarded her a scholarship.

Her mother said, "Good luck."

Rosario did well in school. She discovered she enjoyed the study of parasites and diseases of the lower digestive tract. In 1972 she received a grant to participate in a World Health Organization project improving the living conditions of Brazilian Indians who lived on a tributary of the Amazon. Rosario was excited. She knew the Indians had many stomach problems. She'd never traveled before.

On her way to Brazil she stopped to investigate a viral gastroenteritis study conducted in the Guatemalan highlands. She then went to El Salvador to visit Tomás, a boy she met at her university. Tomás wore his long black hair in a ponytail. He was completing a thesis on Salvadoran agriculture, which, as far as Rosario could tell, consisted mostly of corn.

Once she was south of Mexico, Rosario ate a lot of corn. In Guatemala and El Salvador people didn't eat thin soft tortillas, but thick stiff *gorditas*, corncakes, the size of her palm. Even in the swampy heat of coastal El Salvador, people rose in the morning and drank *atol*, a sweet dense drink made from ground corn. Men sold boiled corn on the streetcorners of La Libertad, the coastal city where Rosario and Tomás stayed. Endless cornfields lined both sides of the sandy road between La Libertad and Zumzal, a small town farther down the coast, where Rosario and Tomás went to eat *arroz valenciana*, a rice dish made with chunks of fish, shrimp, carrots and, of course, bright yellow kernels of corn.

One day Tomás took Rosario to the cornfields to show her, he said, how corn worked. He showed her the male flower, the tassel, at the very top of the stock, and, way down below, the silky female flower that caught pollen blown by the wind. Tomás, Rosario could tell, loved corn as much as she loved parasites. Tomás also loved El Salvador. He grumbled that things in the country weren't right.

Rosario heard other people grumble, too. While Tomás worked on his thesis she lay on La Libertad's black sand beaches and eavesdropped on lithe girls from the capital who sunbathed around her. The government, they complained, had shut down the universities. The government, they said, had arrested the recently elected president and vice president.

Rosario studied her parasitology textbooks. She sipped cold beer. Tomás worked harder on his thesis, sometimes not stopping to eat. One late afternoon Rosario went alone to Zumzal for *arroz valenciana* and stayed too long at the restaurant. She watched the way the sunset shined on shiny black sand. She missed the last bus to La Libertad. It was only seven miles away. She decided to walk.

Twilight is brief at that latitude. Rosario started down the empty road. The sky grew dark. She heard a car approaching slowly behind her. She turned and saw a white Mercedes with a mustached man at the wheel. He drove up beside her. He asked if she needed a ride. "I can take you anywhere you want to go." Rosario said no and kept walking. The man pulled his car in front of her, blocking her way. She turned and ran. She fell. When the man grabbed her and dragged her back to his car, she picked up a handful of sand. With his hands around her neck the man tried to force Rosario into his car. She struggled. She fell. The man kicked her again and again. She watched his snakeskin boot pound her ribs, but she felt nothing.

"Stop," she said. "I'll go with you. I want to kiss you. I want you to fuck me."

He let her stand. She threw her handful of sand into his eyes and dashed deep into the cornfields. The leaves cut her face and hands. She lay down in dirt. She heard the man drive away, and then nothing except the buzzing of a thousand mosquitoes.

Tomás took Rosario to the hospital. He asked her if she would recognize the man if she ever saw him again. And she did, a week later, at the beach, where he sat with a woman and two children. Rosario ran and told Tomás who ran and found his friend Victor, who hunted iguanas and had a rifle.

"Just give me the word," Tomás told Rosario. "We'll kill that rich bastard."

Victor nodded. *"En este parte del mundo, la muerte es banal."* In this part of the world, death is banal.

Rosario looked at Tomás and realized he'd been in El Salvador long enough to absorb the country's ethos. She told Victor to go home. Two days later she left for Brazil.

Tomás stayed on in El Salvador. He wrote Rosario saying that every time he traveled between La Libertad and Zumzal he thought of her. When Rosario returned to the States, Tomás' letters were few. He wrote of massacres and death squads and bodies left to rot by the side of the road. Rosario suggested he leave El Salvador. But in time his letters ceased.

chapter ten

FOR MANY YEARS I couldn't stand the taste of cinnamon and chocolate. During a *Treasure of the Sierra Madre* period of my father's life, he lived in Mexico where he learned Spanish and became an aficionado of Mexican food. In our home hot chocolate wasn't Nestlé, but Ibarra brand chocolate, Mexican-made and spiced with cinnamon. At my father's insistence my mother whipped the chocolate to a froth with a wooden Mexican whisk, a *molinillo*, which he taught her to spin, in the Mexican manner, between her palms. Back then, *gringo* supermarkets didn't sell Ibarra chocolate, so my father bought it in Tijuana when he visited friends who owned souvenir shops on the town's main street.

Although Tijuana, the Mexican border, was thirty minutes from our home, Ibarra's six-sided, red-and-yellow box, its thick chocolate bars wrapped in flimsy white paper, their aroma, seemed exotic to me. I was a fat child. Hot chocolate was always a treat. Handing me a perfumy mug of the stuff, my father told me the Aztecs and their conquerors had loved the combination of cinnamon and chocolate. I loved it, too.

When I was older, in Tijuana I came across the aroma of chocolate and cinnamon—wafting late at night from street vendors' big aluminum pots, or in early-morning working-class restaurants where people sipped their hot chocolate from plastic mugs, the smell mingling with piney disinfectant from freshly mopped floors.

I met Ernie on one of Tijuana's crowded downtown streets. I asked him what he thought about the upcoming election and he laughed. "*No me importa*," I don't care.

I liked his laugh. For whatever reason he liked me. He invited me out for a beer and we became friends and we saw each other often whenever I was in town.

Ernie came from a family of eleven children who had migrated northward from the state of Durango to find work. He was a salesman in a fancy glass-and-marble downtown Tijuana department store that catered to tourists. The store gave him a fifty-percent discount on clothes, so he dressed well, but his salary was low. Most of what he earned he made on commission. During tourist season he was able to provide for his three sisters who lived with him and to send money to his parents in Durango. During the winter, tourists thinned out. He was too proud to let me pay for his beer, so he started inviting me to his home on the outskirts of town. We got off the bus and walked down a cobblestone road that gave out at a shallow gully. Across that gully and up a dirt path, Ernie's house sat at the rise of a steep hill.

In the winter when it rained, the gully churned with red silty water. The dirt path was deep mud. Ernie's sisters always waited for us. When we dried off, they handed us plates of small soft tacos and mugs of Ibarra chocolate. We laughed and ate and watched television. Sometimes we sat and listened to the unhappy couple next door, their voices clear and loud through the wall that separated Ernie's home from theirs.

One winter it rained for weeks. Ernie and I stood on his porch watching the rain course off the corrugated roof, and he said he had to ask me a favor. He stared at the rain and told me he had gotten a girl pregnant, an eighteen-year-old girl who worked at the store's perfume counter.

"We did it only one time," he said. "And she's pregnant and I don't have any money. I need money to take her across the border to an American doctor so she'll be well taken care of and nobody will know she had an abortion."

He named a figure, more money than I had in the world at that time. I suppose I could have borrowed the money, but I didn't know how I felt about paying for an abortion. I told him I had to think about it.

By the time we finished talking, the rain was falling in sheets and you could hear water rushing through the gully. Ernie asked me to spend the night. We all slept in the same room—Ernie's three sisters on the fold-out couch, Ernie and I on a narrow single bed in the corner. After the lights were out, I felt Ernie shake. Very quietly, he cried himself to sleep.

I never loaned Ernie the money. He married the perfume girl. They had another baby. I moved far away and by the time I tracked Ernie down again he was living in a cinder-block house across the gully from where he'd lived with his sisters. His wife had left him with the two kids and run off to Mexico City to become, he said, an actress. Ernie laughed when he told me his story. He was holding Ruby, his baby daughter. I asked him to forgive me for not loaning him the money. I said I was sorry I had ruined his life. He didn't look at me. He looked at his daughter dozing in his arms. "She is the treasure of my life."

I believe he forgave me. But for years I avoided the taste of cinnamon and chocolate. Ernie's son and daughter are now teenagers. He has wrinkles around his eyes. He has a paunch. I do, too. I keep a box of Ibarra chocolate in my kitchen. It isn't easy for me to drink, but I do.

IF YOU'RE BORN AND raised in this part of Southern California, you may remember an old house down near the border. It stood empty for decades. Broken roof tiles. Thick cracks through the foundation. Mice ran in the walls. Every corner reeked of urine. Old orange rinds and cigarette butts littered the floor. A cat skeleton gathered dust in the bathtub. Before it all was bulldozed under, a hand-painted sign hung from the mailbox. The sign said, *Los Solteros*, The Bachelors.

For many years a half-dozen orange trees thrived in the backyard, their thick roots knotted deep in poor soil. After the house was abandoned, it became a hideout for illegal immigrants crossing the border, a few hundred yards away. They'd crouch on the filthy floor, catch their breath. They'd crawl out the back door to the orange trees and fill their pockets with fruit. Inside the house they'd suck the oranges dry and gather courage to dash for a bus, a taxi, any means to get farther north. They never wondered who *Los Solteros* were, the two men who planted the orange trees. I don't think anyone now remembers *Los Solteros*.

Jim descended from the city's Portuguese families who made their fortunes fishing tuna. From his downtown office window, Jim could see the bay: green when choppy, blue when calm. He sat with his back to the view. He was married to a redhead whose life revolved around racing season. (Only Del Mar. She refused to go to Agua Caliente in Tijuana.) Raymond, also a native, came from Dustbowl-era Oklahomans. He taught high school Spanish. He was engaged to a blonde from Fresno who worked as a court reporter.

When Jim wasn't having an affair with a secretary, his office made him claustrophobic. During lunch hour he took long walks. One summer afternoon he found himself at a drugstore where he met Raymond. Jim was paging through a boating magazine. Raymond was reaching for a tennis magazine. Their eyes met.

Not many people back then thought aloud about this sort of thing. Not many could reasonably describe it. Jim and Raymond lived in a part of the world where there were few precedents. When Jim's divorce was final and Raymond's fiancée returned to Fresno, the two men decided to build a home down near the border where, at that time, they could live in privacy.

Orange trees were Raymond's idea. He and Jim spent a weekend or two digging the holes. Their shovels revealed Indian artifacts—knives made of stone, a sort of pipe made from animal bone, seashells. Jim arranged the artifacts atop bookshelves and across window sills. They were the house's only decoration. In time the orange trees took root. They dropped their leaves and their unformed fruit. Jim blamed Raymond for wanting orange trees in the first place. They argued. After the shouting, Raymond stood in the quiet kitchen and stared out the window at the scrawny trees.

We like to say we can grow anything here in Southern

Californa, and for the most part we can. But we live in a desert and we tend to overwater—a particular danger for oranges. They've adapted so well to our region that they like to stay dry, which is why neglected trees are often heaviest with fruit.

Jim overwatered. He'd been overwatering the orange trees on the Sunday morning Raymond found him lying unconscious on the lawn. The garden hose was running full blast. A line of black ants traced its way across Jim's cheek and into his open mouth. The county coroner said, "Heart attack."

Raymond noticed that Jim's secretary behaved with less decorum than is customary at an employer's funeral. She embraced Jim's casket. She kissed its lid. She threw a dozen roses into the grave. Raymond went home and put all of Jim's clothes in a box in the garage. Months later he noticed that the orange trees were looking better.

Raymond didn't stay long at the house. On weekends, it was too quiet. He opened a desk drawer and saw one of Jim's pens. One night, he found one of Jim's tie clasps beneath a cushion on the couch. Raymond waited until the school year ended. He got up on a Saturday morning and wrote and signed the note which for years would trap the house in legal limbo, and incidentally provide refuge and oranges to hundreds of illegal immigrants. The note said, "To Whom It May Concern: I don't want this house." Raymond left the note on the kitchen table. He walked out the back door and headed south toward the border. He kept walking and, as far as anyone ever knew, never looked back.

chapter eleven

THERE ARE MORE GLAMOROUS taco stands in Tijuana. The one I frequent sits on a plaza between the municipal and state government buildings. A father and two sons run the stand. A sad-eyed mutt loiters in its shadow. Light-skinned bureaucrats, and the (almost always) darker-skinned citizens they serve, start crowding the stand around 9:00 a.m. By noon, people press two and three deep against its shiny steel counter. The mutt, full of scraps, dozes.

The elder son plunges long metal tongs into a great pot of beef stewed in red spicy broth. With a cleaver, he minces the meat into a feathery mound. The cleaver's tapping prompts him to sing—which he does, under his breath—love songs, in a soft tenor. "You who were so happy at my side," he sings. *Chop-chop-chop*. "You lacked for nothing." *Chop-chop-chop*. "I'd like to know . . . the reason why . . . our love ended." The cleaver's polka rhythm hypnotizes. Customers stare at the mid-distance, beef broth droplets on their chins.

The younger son stands wordless at his brother's side. He doles out napkins and icy Coca Colas. Before him, a dozen tortillas lie on a sooty black grill, softening in a slick of golden melted lard. The elder brother picks up a tortilla, cups it in his hand, and tucks a spoonful of beef inside it. With a flick of his wrist, he scatters minced onion and cilantro across the beef. With another quick motion, he flicks a spoonful of red salsa into the taco; with another, a dash of broth from the great pot. This process takes five seconds. He sometimes fumbles. A bit of meat, or a tortilla, falls to the ground where it's devoured by the thick-waisted mutt.

I've eaten tacos in Tijuana since I was four or five, when my father would take me down. He went to visit friends. My mother always warned, "Don't let him eat tacos." My father always did. His Tijuana friends—big men with big black mustaches—liked to feed me. They propped me on a stool. They squeezed my chubby thighs. I sat there, gape-mouthed like a hatchling. When my father brought me home, my mother groaned. My breath reeked of onion.

Driving down to Tijuana at night there's a point when the

city comes in view, a field of pinpoint lights. As Tijuana has grown, so has this field grown denser and broader. Some nights fog drifts in from the coast, smearing the lights, blurring the horizon. Tijuana appears to stretch on forever. Now, two million citizens. Whenever the city rises clear or foggy through my windshield, I get bewildered.

"The State Begins Here," says the legend across the entrance to Tijuana's municipal government building. I've never understood its many offices. My favorite is the Office of Administrative Controversies, which, the times I've passed it, has been empty. A few weeks ago I was surprised to see a receptionist at the front desk. I asked what her office did. She looked stricken. She rifled through her desk. She got up and whispered to someone around the corner. She came back, said, "We have a pamphlet that explains everything, but a copy can't be found. Can you perhaps return tomorrow morning?"

I've considered moving to Tijuana, if for nothing more than being closer to my favorite taco stand with its singing older brother. I however lack suspension-of-disbelief. A *gringo,* I take things literally. I fail to read between the lines. In Mexico, I'm oblivious to the joke everyone else is in on. In Mexico, I'm forever the straight man. I tell Mexican friends about my visit to the Office of Administrative Controversies, and they laugh. I'm no different from the gape-mouthed and gullible chubby-thighed boy I was more than forty years ago.

"*Quitate, feo*"—get out of here, ugly—a woman at the taco stand says to the mutt. He looks at her forlornly. People at my taco stand don't talk a lot. They're either bracing themselves to confront Mexican bureaucracy, or they work within its strange administration. I stand outside it all, neither conspirator nor victim. Not long ago, not far from the stand, drug lords assassinated a district attorney.

I order three tacos and a Coke. I wait for the elder brother to sing.

THE LABEL SHOWS A factory. A white one-story building with a red-tile roof and brown smokestack stands beside a beige two-story building. In front of the buildings, on a green lawn, three barrels and two crates lie at odd angles, as if tossed down and then forgotten.

The label appears on thousands of bottles of *aguardiente de cana*, cane liquor, produced in a small town I visit in central Mexico. The town is ninety minutes southeast of Mexico City and thirty miles northwest of Popocatéptl, a large and active volcano that huffs and puffs and lends a sense of futility to human endeavor conducted in its shadow. Fields of sugarcane and sorghum encircle the small town. Local men work in the fields for a few dollars a day. On weekends they drink beer, or cane liquor.

Most rural areas in Mexico produce their own version of *aguardiente*, and, like American moonshine, it's generally considered low-class stuff. Certain states, however, produce fruit-flavored *aguardientes* that even Mexico City sophisticates esteem. Chiapas uses peaches. Puebla, apples. Yucatan, guavas. In the small town I visit, the factory sometimes makes an *aguardiente* flavored with a bitter brown nut gathered in the forest. I've asked what the nut is called. No one seems to know.

The woman I visit is American and some years ago married into the Vivanco family, an artistic clan that's lived in the town for at least a century. The Vivancos have produced a number of well-known painters, sculptors, antiques dealers, and schizophrenics. A few Vivancos live in Paris, a few in New York, a few in Mexico City. Those Vivancos who return or never leave are regarded with affection by the other townspeople. They provide color and excitement.

Near the center of town my friend's brother-in-law, Hector, a carpenter, built a home. On its white plaster facade he mounted a hand-painted tile bearing the words *Casa de Desengaño*, House of Disappointment. Two years ago he was found dead in his living room. He'd been bludgeoned with a bottle of *aguardiente*. The state police ruled his death an "accident."

The Vivancos are fond of their local cane liquor. Luis, Hector's brother, who hangs out near the church, is rarely without a bottle. He was gone for a number of years until, as my friend explained, "he escaped in one of those famous Mexico City asylum escapes. You know, someone opens the doors and all the patients run out into the street." The Vivancos agree that *aguardiente* stabilizes Hector better than any of the medications he was given at the asylum. He occasionally waits in front of the elementary school to corner children and tell them he's going to kill their parents. The children laugh and move on.

The local *aguardiente* is smooth and clear and has a mild vanilla flavor that comes perhaps from the cane. Although forty proof, you can drink a great deal of it without suffering a hangover, which is its first danger. The second is its price—fifty cents a liter or, if you bring your own bottle to the factory, twenty-five cents. Other than the Vivancos and *aguardiente*, the town offers little entertainment.

In the dry season you can go to the hot springs four miles away where the same geological forces that rumble through Popocatéptl pump eighty-degree water into four vast pools. The entrance fee is seventy-five cents. For a little more you can rent a locker, of which there are 560. The times I've visited, I've never seen more than a dozen other people. An old man always sits in a cabaña near the entrance. For a few pesos he'll lop the top off a fresh coconut and fill it with *aguardiente*.

Once when no taxis or busses were available, I left the hot springs on foot. About a mile away, in the middle of nowhere, I came across a squat building that advertised itself as a clinic. Peering through the windows I saw a dusty examination table. Cobwebs trailed from white-enameled medical cabinets. A sign posted on the front door said the clinic was operated by a Dr. Delgado who received his degree in parapsychology from the University of Mexico City. I later called a friend who teaches linguistics there and asked if the school had such a department.

"Perhaps," he said. "The university is so old and so huge, it could have a parapsychology department. Somewhere. I mean, it's entirely possible."

The last time I was in the small town it was a few days after Day of the Dead and the government's volcanologists had upgraded Popocatéptl's status to Code Yellow, which meant an eruption was possible but not certain. My friend and I went to visit Hector's grave, still littered with marigold petals, melted candles, and empty bottles of *aguardiente*. Someone from the Vivanco family had placed a purple papier-mâché dragon's head atop the headstone. I asked my friend why. She shrugged. "That's just the way they are." I would have pressed the point but mosquitoes filled the air and dengue fever is endemic in the area. I suggested we go. As we walked back to my friend's house I asked if she would ever return to America. From the bottom of her street we had a clear view of Popocatéptl, the wreath of cloud around its cone. My friend said she might come back someday, but so far has not made the effort.

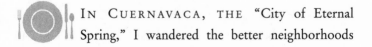 IN CUERNAVACA, THE "City of Eternal Spring," I wandered the better neighborhoods

northeast of the cathedral, browsed the ceramics shops, the pottery shops, and passed Fernanda's chorizo shop.

The mural beside the entrance is a rendering of Xochicalco, a pyramid twenty-four miles to Cuernavaca's south. Painted by Enrique, Fernanda's husband, the mural is so detailed you can see each step leading to the pyramid's summit. You can see the cracks and pits in every stone. What makes the mural memorable isn't its realism, the tropical sunset shimmering in the background, but a scene at the pyramid's top. A Mayan priest, with an arm corded with muscle, holds a knife heavenward. Before him cowers a pig.

Fernanda once considered printing postcards of the mural to sell in her shop. She had second thoughts. It wasn't so much that the priest atop the pyramid was Mayan. (The Maya had penetrated Mexico that far north, and there were anthropologists who believed that the Maya had in fact visited Xochicalco.) It was the pig and the humanlike terror Enrique had rendered in its eyes.

Mexicans make more than one hundred different kinds of chorizo, and the small towns outside Mexico City, like the one Fernanda was from, are known for making the best kinds. Everyone agrees that the pork must be chopped, not ground, and that it must be seasoned with at least chile, paprika, and coriander seed. Of course proportions are open to debate. There's always someone who adds a secret ingredient that produces a chorizo surpassing all others.

Fernanda's hometown was noted for its unfriendliness. At

some point in its history, the inhabitants hit upon sour inwardness as the distinctive quality that would distinguish their town from others in the region. Tourists who found their way to the unattractive market in Fernanda's hometown didn't linger. The fountain at the market's center was broken. Beneath its stagnant green surface, mosquito larvae twitched. The women who ran the market's stalls answered questions with a sneer.

Fernanda, a tall girl from a family of merchants, married Enrique, a thin boy from a family of farmers. Enrique hoped to be an artist. His big break came when the Department of Health commissioned him to paint a mural on the town hall illustrating the prevention of cholera, dengue fever, and syphilis. Two-thirds of the mural were a success. Enrique depicted syphilis, however, as a spiny-tailed devil attacking naked Adam and Eve. Citizens judged this an affront to public morals and immediately white-washed the mural. Disgusted, Enrique swore off murals and took up jewelry making. Fernanda, pregnant, took to making chorizo and selling it in her hometown's market.

Because Fernanda had no particular faith in Enrique's potential, because she was pregnant and needed cash, she was more friendly than the other women in the market. She smiled. Business was slow. The townspeople didn't like her smile and they doubted her chorizo could be better than their own. But it had a mysterious flavor and soon people were buying it out of curiosity. Inevitably a woman from Cuernavaca bought some, too. She told her wealthy friends about the tall girl who sold remarkable chorizo in a small unfriendly town.

Enrique knew that Fernanda's secret was a quantity of powdered cinnamon she mixed into the coarsely chopped pork. He was disgusted that something so simple brought his wife fame. When Fernanda opened her chorizo shop in Cuernavaca, she tried to soften Enrique by asking him to please paint the mural beside the front door. (The idea was that Fernanda's chorizo was an authentic regional product, and what could be more authentic and regional than Xochicalco?) Naturally there were passers-by who said a pig was never sacrificed on a Mexican pyramid. And anyway the animal's frightened humanlike eyes were a scandal. At first Fernanda liked the mural, but in time she saw the pig for what it was.

Fernanda and Enrique had long ago stopped sharing the same bed. They barely spoke at dinner. They were polite to each other only at weddings, baptisms, and funerals.

"We were just children when we married," she said about herself and her husband. She remembered what it was like to love him. She remembered trying to keep her hands away from his face when they kissed. She knew her fingers smelled of cinnamon and pork.

Fernanda was relieved when a large supermarket chain made overtures about her chorizo. The lawyers said her chorizo would be sold in a hundred stores. The Cuernavaca shop would be maintained as a symbol of the product's regional authenticity.

Fernanda has done well by her hometown. She paid to have the market's fountain repaired and cleaned. She buys textbooks and shoes for the poorest children. She has an apartment in Mexico City and a vacation home on a remote Oaxacan coast. She doesn't visit her hometown a lot.

She comes sometimes to Cuernavaca and you might meet her at a cocktail party there. She's stout and matronly. Enrique remains thin. They never speak to each other. The only way you might know they were related is that Fernanda always wears one of Enrique's necklaces, a string of simple stones carved with Mayan glyphs.

chapter twelve

I WENT TO MAHANE YEHUDA, Jerusalem's central market, where I haggled with a spice merchant over the price of dried mint. The merchant refused to lower his price. I walked away. He called after me. Jet-lagged, tired of bickering, I said, "Don't worry. I'm coming back." Everyone around me—shoppers, merchants, delivery boys—roared. A rabbi standing a few feet away laughed so hard he choked. In a very clear and irritated voice I had actually said, "Don't worry. I'm a pig."

I became a Holy City laughingstock because I confused

"come back," *hozer*, with "pig," *hazir*. I was tired. The two words *are* similar. Friends say the spice merchant still remembers me. It's not every day that a Jew stands in the middle of Jerusalem's largest market and calls himself a pig. What made my mistake so hilarious to Israeli ears was that, for many centuries, Jews *were* pigs.

As early as the third Century, Christians fixated on the Jewish refusal to eat pork. Pig-eating was a point of Christian pride, one of the new religion's selling points. A Christian could keep his foreskin and eat pork, too. Over the centuries this enthusiasm for sausage and baby-back ribs segued into ham-fisted hatred for Jews. European folklore explained that Jews did not eat pork because Jews were pigs in disguise. (Jews could not eat themselves.) Jews were dirty and smelly. Like pigs, they could be slaughtered with impunity.

Europe's Jews must have felt they were surrounded by lunatics. The Christian pork obsession was so passionate and persistent, however, that some Jews started taking the fuss seriously. A Talmud scholar in the thirteenth century noted the similarity between the Hebrew words for "come back" and "pig." He wondered if this weren't a clue that, come the Messianic Age, God would "return" the pig to Jews as an animal permissible for consumption.

Christians weren't much interested in pork as a symbol of Jewish liberation. Once it was settled in their minds that Jews were pigs, they set about putting this notion to use. During the Spanish Inquisition, Jews forced to convert to Christianity were called *Marranos*, or swine. The Spanish somehow doubted that any conversion effected through torture could be sincere, and were always dropping in on the *Marranos* to make sure the new converts had pork products on hand. The *Marranos* took to hanging hams outside their front doors and always kept a sausage or two tucked away in a kitchen cupboard, just in case.

In Regensburg, Germany, a carving on the cathedral's exterior depicts Jews suckling a pig's teats. Well into the eighteenth century, one of the gates leading into Frankfurt was decorated with a painted relief showing a Jew sucking shit from a pig's ass. (Pigs, after all, eat their own excrement.) This rather striking image, the *Judensau*, Jew Pig, was popular among the German-speaking peoples. *A Singular Beast*, Claudine Fabre-Vassas' anthropological study of "Jews, Christians, and the Pig," offers reproductions of two German engravings. One from the seventeenth century repeats the scene from the Frankfurt gate; the other, an eighteenth century work, depicts a Jew similarly occupied while the pig nibbles on a human turd.

You don't forget something like that. Even as they fought to establish the State of Israel, there were Jews who remained haunted by the *Judensau*. Fired by dreams of a "New Jew" emancipated not only from Judaism, which had caused Jews so much sorrow, but also from Christian fantasies, they made a point of eating pork on Yom Kippur, the holiest day of the Jewish year.

I have a friend who, on both his mother's and father's side, descends from families that escaped to North Africa during the Spanish Inquisition. In this century they made their way to Montréal. My friend's mother cooked dishes reminiscent of Spain. His father spoke *Ladino*, the Spanish-Hebrew dialect common to Jews whose ancestors fled the Inquisition.

But my friend's sister as a teenager began to complain that her nose was large, that her hair was kinky. She started reading books by Christian author C.S. Lewis. She saved her allowance to have her hair straightened. One evening my friend and his mother went to a movie. When they returned, they heard Handel's "Messiah" blaring from their home. Inside, they found my friend's sister, arms outstretched, kneeling before the living room stereo. My friend says he and his mother laughed out loud.

The next morning they confronted the sort of thing that happens in reality but never in fiction. My friend and his mother woke to the smell of something odd going on in the kitchen. His sister, in her bathrobe, was standing in front of the stove, frying a big pan of Canadian bacon. She went on to become a Christian. Later, while in college, she married a young man who was the son of German immigrants. His father was unapologetic about the fact that he had once belonged to the *Hitlerjugend*, the Nazi youth movement.

Go figure.

MY FRIEND NIANG MARCHES around in black boots and in general projects decisiveness and self-discipline. She lectures on Chinese film at a local university. She swims laps in the university's pool. In a maroon bathing suit, her pale slim body slices through the water. Back and forth, fifty, sixty laps. I've often wondered what she thinks about while she swims. When she's done, she's hungry, and sometimes she calls me and we go out for lunch. When we do, we often talk about food.

Once, before Thanksgiving, we were discussing what our families planned to make for the big dinner. Her American husband, she said, did all the cooking—turkey, stuffing, candied yams. She screwed up her face in disgust when she said "yams."

"My husband says they're part of the Thanksgiving tradition. So. Fine. He can make and eat them. Our son can eat them. I won't. Americans can have these cozy associations with them—home, the holiday, family. I eat them and I think of other things.

"My memories about yam are much more complex than something warm and sweet. Sugar was rare and expensive when I was a little girl growing up in China. Sugar was rationed. In the late 1950s, early '60s, for us the yam functioned as a sugar. It was one of the few sweet-tasting things we had to eat. You roasted yams. You ate rice gruel with yams. You cooked yams, sliced them, dried them in sun. It became like a dried fruit, quite chewy. Dried yam was like a cookie or a candy. We were quite privileged, actually. My father was a professor. We had yams to eat.

"There are very few Chinese in China who don't have some memory of hunger, of times when they had very little or nothing to eat. I grew up right after Mao's Great Leap Forward when he had his crazy plan to turn China into one of the world's greatest producers of steel. People melted down their woks and knives. Everyone ate in communal kitchens. Peasant farmers were forced to join collectives, but no one went to work in the fields and there was famine.

"People now say that twenty, maybe as many as forty million people died of starvation because of the Great Leap Forward. Anhui was one of the worst provinces. Over two million people starved to death there. In one county alone twenty villages were entirely wiped out. There was cannibalism. Dozens of cases of cannibalism in Anhui.

"We were living in Beijing, so we had something to eat. Not much. We ate a lot of yams. And later, during the Cultural Revolution, my father was labeled a 'rightist' and to punish him the government expelled our family from Beijing and sent us to live in Anhui province, where so many people had died of hunger. Anhui was still very poor.

"We were in a small town. Everyone knew about my father. During the Cultural Revolution, people acted like fanatics to show the government that they were loyal. I was a child walking down the street, and people called me names and threw food at me. Food. In a place where thousands of people, only a few years before, had starved to death. There in Anhui people threw food at me to show their disgust, how much they hated me and my family.

"When I was older I was sent to work on a collective farm, and we didn't have much to eat. Rice was very rare. We ate corn meal. Pickled vegetables. Yams. On very important holidays we got some pork fat and that was a real treat. Your body was so hungry for oil and fat. My roommate's family sent her a ceramic jar filled with lard, pork lard, and I can still remember the smell of it. Every night she'd stir a little into her corn meal mush, to give it some flavor, to have some fat in her diet.

"We had very little to eat, but we still had to work. We grew rice. I stood for many hours in rice paddies, planting rice, up to my thighs in cold water. My doctor thinks that's why I have an arthritis condition in my legs, from the bad nutrition, from all those days I spent standing in cold water. So, I'm still a relatively young woman and I swim to keep myself strong, to keep myself limber.

"When I went back to China last year I was surprised to see that they were still selling roasted yams on street corners. For the younger people, it's something nostalgic. It reminds them of their childhood. Three times I tried to eat yam, and I couldn't. I couldn't. My childhood was very different.

"Eighteen years ago, when I first came to this country it was before Thanksgiving and I went to the supermarket with

109

my husband. He was buying all these things and he said, 'Oh, we can't forget yams.' And I had this very violent reaction. I was very confrontational. I was almost angry. I said, 'What do you want to buy *those* for?' And he just stood there. He couldn't understand why I was so upset.

"You love someone and you marry them and you think you know everything about them and then there are times when you realize that there are things they can't possibly know or understand about you. I'm Chinese and in China making a beautiful meal for someone is the highest expression of love. Food is a very sensual, passionate thing. Culturally, I understood why my husband wanted to make this big meal for me. But he couldn't understand why I was having such a strong reaction to such a silly simple thing like yams.

"It's hard to understand how something that tastes sweet in one person's mouth, in another person's mouth can taste so bitter."

SOMETIME IN MID-AUGUST my train pulled into Turin. I could see Aliza at the end of the platform, waiting just beyond the turnstile. She was a pale girl, her red hair cut into a blunt pageboy. She wore a white linen dress. She saw me and waved. Hot Italian light glinted off the gold bracelet she wore on her thin left wrist. I ran toward her down the platform. I thrust my sweaty face at her for a kiss. She turned so my mouth met her cheek.

We hadn't seen each other for a while. We'd met nine months before in Jerusalem at a conference sponsored by the World Union of Jewish Students. Aliza was representing an Italian-Jewish students organization. I was working for the World Union's campaign for Soviet Jewry. Together we attended an interminable meeting. Jewish students from around the world screamed at each other and bickered. They scalded one another with sarcasm, the Jewish lingua franca. At one point Aliza and I glanced at each other. We both laughed out loud. We rose from the table and staggered out to the hallway where we slapped our thighs and hooted. When our laughter died down we'd look at each other and laugh some more. She was very pretty, I thought.

We corresponded, Aliza and I. Cautious letters. "I couldn't stop thinking about you after I left Jerusalem," she wrote. "Why don't you come visit me in Turin? You can meet my parents."

Our plan was to meet at the Turin station and drive north to her family's summer home in the Valle d'Aosta, a strange French-speaking part of Italy near the Alps. Our trip was uneventful. Aliza didn't say much. She played a cassette of Italian punk rock. One song, which I remember well, featured a male vocalist again and again hollering in English, "Don't touch my brain!" Aliza seemed to find the song soothing.

When we reached her parents' vacation home, a 200-year-old chalet of wood and stone, two people burst from the front door and, with something like ecstasy, dragged me and my luggage from the car.

"I hope you've come to stay for a long time!" the father said.

"Yes!" cried the mother. "Stay as long as you want!"

We had lunch in the garden. It was the best meal I've ever eaten. Aliza's mother placed on the table a cold veal roast, a bottle of dark green olive oil, and a wooden bowl of brilliant red tomatoes Aliza's father had grown beside the house. Maybe the clear alpine sunlight and the valley's pure water made the tomatoes so good. Maybe it was my pleasure at seeing Aliza. The tomatoes were unlike any I'd tasted before. Italians grow few eating tomatoes. Their most popular varieties are used for making sauce.

Aliza's father's were round and very sweet. The skins' pungent green aroma lingered on my fingers. They may have been San Marzano tomatoes or Borgeses. I must have eaten a half-dozen with nothing more than olive oil and salt. Aliza's father waded into his garden to pluck more. Aliza eyed me and smiled. She sipped her lemonade.

Aliza's mother served more fresh tomatoes with dinner. More were on the breakfast tray she placed beside my bed the next morning. Aliza's father even tucked some into the picnic basket she and I took on our little driving excursion around the valley. The picnic basket sat on the backseat of her car and as we drove, the air grew hot, and ripe tomato smell drifted to the front seat where I tried, unsuccessfully, to hold her hand. She was again playing "Don't Touch My Brain." The hellish drums, anguished guitar, and lunatic wailing made her pensive.

For our picnic we drove to a park, but it was occupied by a chapter of the Italian Communist Party holding some kind of summer camp. A banner strung above a makeshift stage announced an "International Children's Day." Aliza and I sat in her stuffy car, the engine running, and watched a group of Italian children dressed as Zulu warriors and Chinese peasants stumble through a folk dance. "Don't Touch My Brain" played softly on the car's stereo.

"I love him," Aliza said.

"Who?"

My eyes searched for my rival among the Italian Communists.

"Him! Him!" She pointed at the cassette deck.

"Don't touch my brain!" the nitwit, whoever he was, shouted again.

"I met him two weeks ago. It was too late to tell you not to come. My parents don't like him. It is a scandal."

One of the tiny Zulu warriors threw himself down on the stage and sobbed. I wondered if Communist internationalism extended to Americans in need of a quick ride to Turin.

I left the Valle d'Aosta the following morning. Aliza's parents begged me to stay. She drove me to Turin. When she dropped me off at the station I didn't turn back to wave good-bye. I boarded my train and went to Nice and from there flew on to Jerusalem. I can no longer remember Aliza's face. When I think of the Alps, I don't think of shepherds or the Matterhorn or snow, of even of Aliza. I think of a wooden bowl filled with the sweetest ripe tomatoes.

chapter thirteen

I WAS LIVING IN SOUTH Jerusalem that autumn. The
rain promised by God in Deuteronomy 28 did not fall in its
proper time. Small praying mantises I'd never seen before
dawdled in the corners of the bus shelter nearest my home. The
sky was always a strange gauzy blue. One morning a three-inch-
long cockroach, shiny legs askew, appeared in the bathtub. How
did it get into our sixth-floor apartment? We never knew.

There were other signs and wonders.

"I want a divorce," Leah told me. "I want to go back to
Australia."

I rented a room from Leah and Marc. They'd met in Jerusalem and had been married for ten years. They were part of the large contingent of English-speaking immigrants who lived in Jerusalem at that time. We all knew each other, bickered with and married one another. Marc and I were best friends.

Leah made me promise I wouldn't tell Marc she wanted to leave. She would, she said, tell him herself. Day after day news came of Iraqi troops along the Kuwaiti border. American military advisors were seen in the bars and cafés around the King David Hotel. Letters from Australia, or America, that usually took weeks to arrive, appeared in our mailboxes three or four days after they were sent.

Events around us sped up; our daily lives seemed to slow. Days and nights, especially nights, seemed unusually long. Leah bided her time. On nights that Marc worked late, Leah and I listened to the BBC while she taught me to cook. We made complicated things that took hours to prepare— dumplings filled with minced lamb, phyllo-dough pastries. We stuffed grape leaves, dozens of grape leaves, with rice, mint parsley, dried apricots, and onion. We stuffed grape leaves until our fingertips puckered from the brine in which the grape leaves were packed.

Those evenings we never talked much. The steady business, we understood, kept us occupied until we could go to sleep and get up the next morning and go to work. We cooked carefully, meticulously. We rolled up the grape leaves into neat little cylinders. There in the steamy kitchen, grape leaves simmering on the stove, BBC fading in and out on the short-wave, we had the appearance of coziness and purpose. Sometimes Leah sighed. I wondered when she was going to tell Marc. I knew the day would come, sooner than later.

The week 150,000 Iraqi troops invaded Kuwait, Leah's father in Melbourne was diagnosed with cancer. I almost felt relieved when I went with Marc and Leah to the airport. Security was tight. A lot of plainclothes police in bulky Israeli sportscoats stood around the lobby. They carried briefcases we all knew contained Uzis. It wasn't a time for long good-byes. Marc and Leah embraced in front of the escalator that went up to the departure lounge. Leah turned to me and smiled and up she went.

None of us had much money. The cheapest way of getting from Israel to Australia was to take a Greek jet that stopped not only in Athens and Los Angeles, but in five Asian cities on its way down south. The entire trip took three days. The lay-over in Athens alone was twelve hours. Leah had said she didn't mind the long trip. She said it gave her time to think.

I was at home with Marc the night Leah called from Melbourne and said she was never coming back. Marc's face went white. Sitting at the kitchen table, I pretended to study a brochure explaining how to give yourself an injection of nerve-gas antidote. Weeks passed. Eventually bombs rained down on Baghdad and all our lives changed some more.

One day I got a postcard from Leah that she'd sent while waiting in Athens. She said she'd spent the day wandering through shoe stores. Something about that image stayed in my mind. Leah, a Hungarian girl, with long red hair that fell to her waist. The bright white buildings. The blue Greek sky. Walking down the dusty, noisy streets of a city she doesn't know, walking away from a ten-year marriage she could no longer endure. The postcard—I still have it somewhere—showed the turquoise shallows off an unidentified stretch of Greek coast. I see that brilliant water, and that white, foreign city, when I imagine Leah walking slowly, killing time.

Marc and Leah have each remarried. Marc and his new wife have two kids. Leah and her husband, who owns a radio station, live in a bohemian part of Sydney. I hear from her occasionally. When times are hard, I still make her stuffed grape leaves, which is more useful than pouring myself a drink or taking a pill.

OFF A SMALL SIDE street in downtown Jerusalem, there was a kosher vegetarian restaurant named Alumah's. In the foyer you often saw a young Orthodox girl seated at a table equipped with a white tablecloth, reading lamp, and free-standing magnifying glass. By her modest dress, you knew the girl was *frum*, or religious, but her manner was provocative. Peering through the magnifying glass, she picked through lentils scattered before her across the white cloth. Her fingers darted through the lentils, flicking some—*plink! plink!*—into a bowl in her lap, culling others into a pile to one side of the table. The girl was a living advertisement for the restaurant's religious rigor. She was searching for bugs.

The Biblical prohibition against eating insects is as unequivocal as the prohibition against eating pork or shellfish —a mealworm or mite being the spiritual equivalent of a minute pig or lobster. Orthodox Jews spend considerable time sifting through flour, picking through walnuts and pulses and rice, examining each leaf in a head of lettuce or bunch of spinach, searching for creatures God has forbidden them to consume. Orthodox Jews who eat only organic insecticide-free vegetables—there are a fair number of Orthodox Jewish-Americans who adopt this additional stricture—keep busy kitchens.

There are exceptions. The Talmud allows Yemenite Jews to eat a certain kind of locust. Jewish law requires no Jew to worry about microscopic insects. Miniscule bugs often burrow beneath the skins of cashews and almonds, but if the nuts are roasted until brown "the intensity of the heat," one rabbi wrote, "will dry out the insects to such an extent that they will be regarded as dust and cease to be forbidden."

To non-Jews, even to secular Jews, this attention to detail appears pathological. But if you've handed over your life to holiness, then spending twenty minutes combing through a head of romaine isn't crazy. It is part of the life you lead. It's an expression of love.

Having spent time in the more rigorous reaches of Orthodox Judaism, I can recognize the tiny blister at the edge of a lentil that means a worm has burrowed inside. I can recognize the fine webs in a package of flour that indicates the presence of weevils or, in Yiddish, *milben*. With a magnifying glass I've scrutinized feathery dill for pinhead-size bug eggs. In the big secular world I'm comfortable with fanatical wine connoisseurs, with purists who use only the most virgin first-cold-pressed olive oil and who insist on the superiority of free-range roasting hens.

I'm familiar with the gamut of reasons people choose to eat or drink some things and refuse others. It's been a long time since Jerusalem was my home. I still can't face a package of lentils without trepidation. I ate so many when I was young and poor and in love with God, or at least young and poor and in love with the idea of being in love with God. Each lentil I ate I inspected by hand.

While I know the secular world's sensitivities to food, I also know the awareness isn't reciprocal. I don't expect a *Gourmet* magazine subscriber to have read the story of Esau and Jacob in the original Hebrew, to know how the muddy, meaty taste of lentils evokes a narrative of betrayal. But I am someone who culled lentils and I know how Jacob, with lentils, cheated hairy Esau of his birthright. Esau and Jacob's story ends with ambiguous kisses and hugs. I sometimes wish my own peculiar family drama would achieve similar resolution. I no longer inspect lentils under a magnifying glass, but in my mind's eye they still are huge.

ARAK, AS I KNOW it, is a clear powerful liquor distilled from grapes and flavored with anise. But *arak*'s origins are obscure: names and meaning can change over time. Almost everyone agrees that the word *arak* derives from the Arabic for "sweat." Charles Perry, editor of the *Los Angeles Times* food section and part-time Arabist, explained that *arak* got its name "from the way alcohol condenses in the cooling pipe of a still. It looks like sweat. Medieval Italy apparently came up with the idea of distilling alcohol, but the Arabs swiftly introduced it to Asia." However, Daniel Rogov, food columnist for the *Jerusalem Post*, states that an anise-flavored liquor called *arak*, made from distilled palm wine, first appeared in the Arab Mediterranean 2500 years ago.

Arak is now found all over the world. In Turkey, *raki*. In Yugoslavia, *rakiji*. In Tunisia, *boukha*. In France, *pastis*. A friend of mine born in Madras says rural peasants in southern India drink something called *arak* that they distill from sugarcane. I first began drinking *arak* while studying at a yeshiva in Jerusalem. I didn't have to distill it myself. It was sold in every corner market in Jerusalem and was cheap. During winter, drinking *arak* was a good way to keep warm in the yeshiva's unheated dorm. One Sabbath evening, when a rabbi smelled *arak* on my breath, he clucked his tongue and told me his wife used *arak* to clean windows and mirrors. "It doesn't leave a single streak," he said.

I drank a lot of *arak* with Robert, a theoretical physics student from Toronto. Like most of us at the yeshiva, Robert was new to Orthodox Judaism. He was a genius. He was thin and blue-eyed and had a voice like a dentist's drill. His familiarity with the universe's inner workings, the forces that charged subatomic particles and caused galaxies to wheel through infinite space, made his acceptance of faith difficult. There either was a God, or the universe was pointless. There was either meaning or chaos. On and on he argued with himself, with our rabbis, and with me, who came to faith less arduously, which was, perhaps, my downfall.

I never tired of Robert. Watching him struggle with God was like watching a one-man recapitulation of Jewish history from the Enlightenment to the present. But Robert's struggle had suspense. It wasn't clear if God or science would win. The turning point came, I think, when Robert and I went to the holy city of Tsfat in northern Israel. Robert had become interested in *kabbala*, Jewish mysticism, and many famous Jewish mystics were buried in Tsfat. One night we in our heavy parkas sat sipping *arak* on a hill above the kabbalists' graveyard and watched small blue candles flicker on their headstones. The idea of mysticism—faith at its most cryptic and irrational—rattled Robert. He became agitated. He became angry. The *arak* loosened his tongue. He railed against the millions of Jews who had died for their faith. For what? For superstition?

Our bottle of *arak* clenched in one hand, he raised a fist in the air, "Either there is a God, or Judaism is the cruelest joke that's ever been pulled on any people in the history of the world!"

He had a point. But he wasn't satisfied. He said he wished he could be like me, someone who "just accepted things without question." I told him he couldn't base his faith on what other people did or didn't believe. I had a lump in my throat. I'd had too much *arak*. I was dizzy. Maybe it was the cold wind that made my eyes water. I said, "You can't depend on me or anyone else. What would you do if I stopped being religious tomorrow? What would that prove? You have to make your own decisions."

Not long after we returned to Jerusalem, Robert stopped calling himself Robert (a name, he explained, from the Old High German meaning "bright fame") and began using his Hebrew name, Yerachmiel, which meant "God will have mercy." About the same time, he started giving me his clothes. "They're too big," he said, "The yeshiva food is awful and I've lost weight." I began wearing his jeans and college sweatshirts. He started wearing a yarmulke and the white dress shirt, black slacks and blazer that all serious yeshiva boys wore. Finally he announced he wasn't returning to Toronto to finish his Ph.D.

in physics, but was going to upstate New York to study full time at a yeshiva in Monsey.

We drank *arak* together only one other time. I'd gone back to California where Yerachmiel tracked me down and invited me to his wedding. He wanted me to come to Monsey and be his *shomer*, his "guard," a kind of Jewish "best man" who takes care of the groom before the wedding. (According to tradition, grooms are so addled they can easily lose things or hurt themselves.) When Yerachmiel met me at JFK, he noticed I no longer wore a yarmulke, but he said nothing. He hugged and kissed me. He rubbed my bare head and laughed.

The night before his wedding we sat in a Monsey motel room and drank a little *arak*. He told me how his marriage had been arranged through a *shadchan*, a matchmaker. Although he had yet to touch or kiss Hannah, his bride-to-be, he was very much in love. They'd spent many chaste evenings eating kosher pizza, getting to know each other. Hannah had been religious all her life, he said, "But it doesn't matter to her that I was ever called Robert."

chapter fourteen

POISON HAS FALLEN out of favor. Criminologists aren't sure why. Some say effective poisons in their purest form aren't as available as they once were. A century ago, arsenic and strychnine were household staples. Housewives soaked flypaper in arsenic. Their husbands pumped strychnine into wasps' nests. Every now and then, in a pest-free home, a husband complained that his soup tasted funny, or a wife died suddenly of unexplained causes. Law enforcement lacked the technology to prove anything shady had happened.

Advances in forensic science have made poisoning unwise; the advent of no-fault divorce and restraining orders have, in almost all instances, made it unnecessary. Intentional poisoning has become so rare in America that there's only one toxicologist I'm aware of who makes it his specialty. This Austin-based gentleman flits about the country advising detectives on hard-to-crack cases. He's managed to compose a profile of today's "typical poisoner," a person he describes as "well-educated and immature," in other words, someone much like me.

I've never wanted to kill anyone, but I have wanted to shut someone up. My apprenticeship was slow, my methods simple.

Like most competent cooks, my skills were over time enlisted by family, friends, co-workers. Like most competent cooks, I found myself cooking less often for my own pleasure and more for the pleasure of people I either didn't know well, or knew altogether too well. During many dinners I sat and watched greasy lips pronounce banalities, casual insults. I watched people who claimed not to like red meat devour leg of lamb. I watched people who claimed to dislike sweets devour cheesecake. I tried to escape to the kitchen. Shouts of, "What are you doing in there? Come back and sit down!" forced my return. I developed detachment. I noticed that heavy meals had a sedative effect. Pot roast and mashed potatoes, but not baked sole and coleslaw, quieted people down. Pot roast and mashed potatoes followed by pound cake and ice cream lulled people into drowsy silence punctuated by, "Well, it's about time we went home."

For a while I pondered this phenomenon. I browsed medical journals. By the time my father's terminal cancer rolled around, I was well prepared. My father's slow death meant spending weeks in close quarters with my sister-in-law, an opinionated woman with a healthy appetite and a hyena-like laugh. She had a shaky grasp of inheritance law and, while my mother, brother, and I were occupied with my father's care, she'd wander around my parents' home, examining their furniture.

One afternoon she drew me aside. "You know, the only thing of your parents' that I've ever wanted is that cherry-wood china closet."

I explained that my father was dying, that my mother, as far as I knew, was in good health.

I immediately went to the supermarket and bought a couple hundred dollars worth of groceries, including the resentful cook's best friend, several pounds of butter.

At 100 calories per tablespoon, butter is less caloric than other fats. (Canola oil has 130 calories per tablespoon, olive oil 120.) But butter incorporates itself easily into most foods and its "buttery rich goodness" makes almost everything taste better. Years of cooking and quiet observation taught me, for example, that a pot of mashed potatoes containing two tablespoons of butter didn't taste as good as a pot containing eight. A pot containing twenty-four tablespoons—the most I ever attempted—tasted best of all.

In addition to improving flavor, there are two reasons for

getting as much butter as possible into food, particularly starches. The human digestive system, struggling with an onslaught of hard-to-digest fatty acids, engorges itself with blood the body would otherwise use to keep the mind alert and chatty. Also, butter contains tryptophan, an amino acid which, when absorbed by the brain, induces sleepiness. The trick is getting tryptophan from the gut to the brain. And starches, for complex reasons, accelerate and enhance this process. In the right hands, mashed potatoes can be as calming as Haldol.

Turkey and bananas are also rich in tryptophan. While my father lay dying and my sister-in-law studied her *Beginner's Guide to Antique Appraisal*, I made many loaves of buttery banana bread. I baked a twenty-pound turkey, first rubbed well with unsalted butter. While I was at it, I made stuffing. My recipe from *Joy of Cooking* called for only one cup of melted butter, but I knew that three cups yielded a superior result. I of course made plenty of mashed potatoes.

My mother, brother, and I were too busy and too tired to eat much of this food. Mostly, my mother drank the Ensure my father left untouched beside his bed. My brother and I drank coffee and, on difficult nights, bourbon. My sister-in-law, who didn't have a good intuitive feel for bedpans, oxygen tanks, or morphine pumps, had a lot of time on her hands. In the morning I'd see her slathering butter on a thick slice of toasted banana bread. In the afternoon and evening she'd heat herself up some turkey and mashed potatoes in the microwave. The house grew quiet. There were days I didn't see her much at all. She always seemed to be taking naps.

"LITTLE DEBBIE DOESN'T like to give interviews," said her father, Ellsworth McKee, board chairman and chief administrative officer of McKee Foods Corporation. When I reached Mr. McKee at his Chattanooga home, he was evasive about his daughter whose image has appeared for forty years on thousands of boxes of cookies and snack cakes.

"That little picture of her is how she looked when she was four and a half," he allowed. "Over the years we've changed the hair some, but not so much that anyone would notice."

Studying Little Debbie's image, I saw a smiling auburn-haired girl in a white hat and checkered blue blouse. "Is Little Debbie married? Does she have children? A profession?"

"No. No. And no."

Did she ever work?

Mr. McKee paused. He cleared his throat. "She managed the plant for a while."

Mr. McKee, a Southern gentleman, was trying hard to be polite with me. Whatever was behind his reticence, I'd never know.

Little Debbie is America's leading snack cake brand, with a

line of twenty products and annual sales in excess of $850 million. At the supermarket, I'd seen Little Debbie's Swiss Cake Rolls, Devil Squares, Banana Twins. The packaging's stark simplicity, the fact that almost everything had the same white, intensely sweet "creme" filling, made it all seem redneck. Little Debbie's products reminded me of Moon Pies, another Chattanooga innovation, two cookies, chocolate icing, marshmallow filling.

I knew that my downstairs neighbor, Melanie, was from Chattanooga. The day after my unsuccessful call to Ellsworth McKee, I asked Melanie if she was familiar with Little Debbie.

"Ooooh," she said. "I love Little Debbie's Oatmeal Creme Pies. I ate a whole box the last time I filed for divorce."

I invited her up to my place for a glass of wine and to talk about Little Debbie. Melanie sat ramrod straight in her chair.

"I had to wear a back brace when I was a little girl," she explained. "Because I had curvature of the spine. One metal rod up the front, two up the back, and a big plastic collar to hold up my chin. I was a plump little girl and that back brace fit tight. I had to wear the goddamn thing twenty-three hours a day for four years. Much of that time I just craved the feeling of having that brace off my body. This was when all my girlfriends were starting to notice boys and have crushes. The back brace wasn't very attractive.

"So, to keep my mind off things, I ate a lot of Oatmeal Creme Pies. They're just two oatmeal cookies with a marshmallow filling, but they're so good. I had a friend, Betsy Bare, who was two years younger than me. I'd go over to Betsy Bare's house and she'd play the piano and we'd eat Oatmeal Creme Pies and sing Elton John songs. The piano keys got real sticky.

"Once a week my sister Laurenda would have me over to her apartment to spend the night. She was fourteen years older than me. Real tall. Straight brown hair. Beautiful. She'd have me over and first we'd stop at McCullum's, this little convenience store there in Chattanooga, and she'd buy me whatever I wanted. I always wanted two boxes of those Oatmeal Creme Pies. We'd take 'em back to Laurenda's place and just sit around and giggle and eat all we wanted. The most wonderful thing was that Laurenda let me take off my back brace. She let me keep it off the entire time I was with her. I remember how cool and light my body felt.

"This didn't last forever. Laurenda was having an affair with a much older man, Dr. Geddes, who was very prominent in Chattanooga society. I guess their relationship was rocky. I remember she'd call my mom and cry. Mama didn't like to talk about it. She and my father were ashamed that their daughter was having an affair with a much older man. They lived in fear that people at our church would find out.

"I remember the evening my mother got the call from the hospital over in Douglas County. I was doing dishes with my mother when she answered the phone. They said Laurenda had been shot. They said she was dead. I remember that all of a sudden it felt like my back brace got real tight, like it was going to crush me. I couldn't breathe. I loved Laurenda so much.

"It seems she and Dr. Geddes had gone to spend the weekend at some house he owned out in the country. Dr. Geddes told the police that there'd been an argument, that she'd gone up to his room and taken a shotgun and somehow shot herself under her left breast. He threw her body in the back of his pickup and drove her to the hospital. There was no investigation. The autopsy was rushed. As far as everyone was concerned, Laurenda killed herself. It destroyed my parents. They'd lost a daughter. They were humiliated that everyone in Chattanooga knew about Laurenda and Dr. Geddes. They never pressured the police. They wanted it all to remain a secret. But Chattanooga back then was a small town, and in small towns people talk. A year later, my daddy sold his business and we packed up everything and came to California.

"I'll tell you a secret. I sometimes call Dr. Geddes. Call him late at night. His wife always picks up the phone. I take my time. I whisper real slow, 'I'm sorry to wake you, Mrs. Geddes. I know you don't know who I am. But tell me, Mrs. Geddes, does the doctor sleep well at night?'"

A FLOOR FAN FILLS my office with white noise. At night I leave doors and windows open. The air is so dry I don't sweat. I lie on white sheets and listen to a cricket hiding in the kitchen.

I've lived a long time in Southern California. The autumn Santa Ana still surprises me. I wake up. My sinuses ache. Sparks arc between my fingertips and the bathroom door-knob. Crows loiter in my neighbor's persimmon tree, inky silhouettes against the blue sky. Termites swarm and discard wings on my windowsills. My skin itches. My mouth is always dry. The basil in the garden goes to seed and withers.

"If you can run for thirty minutes, you can run for an hour. If you can run for an hour, you can run for ninety minutes." A friend gave me this advice the fall I returned to San Diego after my marriage ended. My friend had run marathons. I started to run at night because it gave me something to do. "Drink lots of water. Keep yourself hydrated. That's the important thing."

It was an unusually hot and dry autumn. I was in a one-bedroom apartment with no furniture, a computer, many unpacked boxes. I bought myself a pair of running shoes. I ran and ran in the dry night air until my lungs ached and my mouth tasted of copper. I came home. I drank tap water from plastic jugs I kept in my white refrigerator.

I ran on the sidewalk until my shins ached and my friend said I needed to run on a more forgiving surface. I joined a twenty-four hour gym. I started going late at night when I could occupy a treadmill for as long as I wanted. I lugged chilled water with me.

I'd go to the gym after midnight. I bribed an attendant with a twenty-dollar bill to show me how to override a treadmill's sixty-minute limit. I wanted to run for two hours, undisturbed, without the machine beeping at me or stopping. The room of fifteen treadmills faced a bank of six televisions tuned to the same channel. Many nights I was alone. I stared at the televisions. I listened to my breathing. After seven and a half miles, my sweaty tank top grew dry and stiff with salt. I could think only about water. Thirst eclipsed other preoccupations. The trick was to keep running, to sustain my parched isolation for as long as possible. Run ten miles, I told myself, and you can drink all the water you want. Water so cold it burns.

One night at the gym, I noticed a young woman. She was panting on a treadmill on the other side of the room. She was pretty. Blonde. In her early twenties. Flat-chested. She wore a pale blue leotard. The skin across her chest was taut and tan: I could see her clavicle. The night she ran on a treadmill in front of me I saw she had a young boy's ass. And there was a gap at the top of her thighs. My arms were larger than her thighs. As she ran her damp leotard revealed her ribs. One night before her run she knelt beside her treadmill and carefully spooned four tablespoons of Gatorade into a liter bottle of water. She saw me watching. She smiled.

She ran fast, her legs a spidery blur. She'd sprint for ten minutes, hop off the treadmill, take a few sips of Gatorade-spiked water, hop back on. This went on for an hour. I told the night attendant, "The skinny blonde's going to drop dead." He shrugged, snapped his chewing gum. "See it all the time. We can't order 'em out of the gym until they faint from exhaustion."

The night she fell I was watching the televisions. A cartoon bear chased a cartoon rabbit. With a weak little cry, the blonde dropped. Instead of surrendering to the treadmill's momentum, let it slide her back onto the floor, she fought against it, scrambling on her hands and knees. Finally, she gave in. The treadmill pushed her to the floor where she lay, a damp heap. I went to her and knelt beside her, my hand on her shoulder. I could feel bone. I offered her water. "Don't touch me!" she howled. "Don't fucking touch me."

She got up, limped from the room. Our empty treadmills spun crazily. On the televisions, the bear chased the rabbit.

I tried to run a few more nights at the gym, but even my dry mouth, my longing for water, couldn't make me forget the blonde. In my mind I kept seeing her fall. I saw her self-starvation as a parody of my self-imposed drought. The treadmill's steady thrum no longer comforted me. I started to run just before sunset at the beach. I still do. There's a fair number of us, middle-aged, sweating, making our solitary way up and down the coast. To one side of us, acres of dry sand. To the other side, the endless, undrinkable sea.

chapter fifteen

NOT LONG BEFORE DALIA died she sent me to buy a bottle of Château d'Yquem.

"It'll be nice," she said. "We can sit out on the patio and drink it."

Her nurse and I exchanged glances. Dalia reached into a drawer beside her bed and pulled out a wad of twenties.

"Don't give me any guff. Just do as you're told."

I had trouble finding the wine and by the time I returned to Dalia's, the nurse had bundled her up and trundled her out to the patio. The steel rod in Dalia's spine held her upright in her wheelchair. She'd put on lipstick. Her hair had been combed up and back and pinned into a bun. Beneath her blanket and frilly robe, cancer ate at her bones.

I was nervous. I left the expensive wine in the freezer too long and it almost froze. Dalia didn't mind. She sipped her glass only once or twice after I poured it. She stared at her garden a long while.

In a distracted voice she said to me, "You're going to be just fine."

Dalia was an old friend of my family's. She'd encouraged my parents to send me to school overseas. When they balked, she underwrote my education. She pushed me out into the world. She also sent me spending money. Addressed in a flowery old-fashioned cursive, the envelopes contained fifty dollars. "Go buy yourself some underwear and socks," her notes said. Or, "Go get yourself a haircut. You probably look like a wild animal."

She also gave me my first taste of Château d'Yquem, there in her living room with its big fireplace, big couches, and big black standard poodle named Cocoa. Dalia liked me, I think, because I listened to her stories about the war, how her family had escaped Lithuania.

"The only good thing about the Russians," she told me, "was when they marched in. They were real bastards. They were drunk and they were violent. You knew what they were up to. The Nazis, well, at first they were polite."

The night she handed me my first glass of Yquem, she said, "You'll learn to like it."

The clear, honey-colored wine was sweet, and unlike anything I'd ever tasted. I never thought anything sweet could be so complicated.

"Can you taste it?" she asked. "That funny taste. Very faint. It tastes like fresh honeycomb."

The "funny taste" in my glass of sweet Yquem was *pourriture noble*, noble rot, what the French call the fungus *Botrytis cinera* when it infects grapes in southwestern France. Elsewhere, when the fungus attacks pears or strawberries, there is nothing noble about it and it's called gray rot. South of Bordeaux, in the Graves region, wine makers hope *pourriture noble* will infect their vineyards. *Botrytis* shrivels the fruit, concentrating character and sugar. Crush the diseased grapes and they yield famous sweet white wines like Chateau d'Yquem, the finest.

Botrytis is fickle. Some years it sweeps through acres of grapes. Other years it dawdles among the vines, granting wrinkly nobility to only a few. There are years it never visits at all and Count Alexandre de Lur-Saluces, maker of Chateau d'Yquem, rises each grim morning to confront acres of healthy grapes. When *Botrytis* does strike, wine makers like the Count play a waiting game: the more rotten the grape, the better the vintage. But if the wine makers delay their harvest too long, until early November, say, rain can drench the fields and make the grapes plump, bland, useless. This test of nerve sometimes pays off. Properly botrytized Yquem sells for $300 per bottle and more.

"I'm tired," Dalia said the afternoon we sat on her patio. "I need to rest. Finish your wine, then come say good-bye."

The nurse wheeled her to her room, helped her into bed, tucked the blankets around her. I stood in the doorway, trying to think of what to say. I wanted to say thank-you, but didn't know how. I thought I still had plenty of time, that "thank you" might sound too final. I thought "thank you" could wait until the last minute.

Dalia looked up. "Don't just stand there looking pitiful. Go out dancing or something. Go take a girl out to dinner."

Every fall I drive out to where Dalia is buried. I can never remember where her headstone is. I'm always surprised when I finally find it. As a belated thank-you, I trim the grass from around the stone, brush the dust from the engraved letters of her name.

"Sin in haste," Dalia always said, "repent at leisure."

I've taken my time. Twenty years have passed. I still miss her.

"In the small village I'm from," she told me the night I first tasted Château d'Yquem, "we had a very old custom. On a child's first day of school, the rabbi would give him a slate on which the first two letters of the Hebrew alphabet were written in honey. The rabbi asked the child to lick up the letters and go on to use the slate to learn to read and write. The child would always remember that learning was sweet like honey."

THE WOMAN WAS IN her early forties. Long brown hair. Blue jeans. Cotton blouse. Sandals. On the front porch where she stood she kept Boston ferns, a few begonias.

She eyed me. "Can I help you?"

I explained that I grew up in the house she now occupied. I said I'd played on the porch where she now stood. I explained that I'd just bought a house, as luck would have it, a few blocks away. I said I'd wanted to see how my old home looked.

"You standing there like that, staring at my house," she said, loudly, as if she wanted neighbors to hear. "It makes me uncomfortable. It's inappropriate. If you don't leave I'm going to call the police."

I thought it was inappropriate that she'd torn out my mother's roses. I thought the squirrel-shaped wind chimes she'd strung across the porch were inappropriate, too. But I smiled. I apologized. I left her with her ferns, begonias, and wind chimes.

I wanted to tell her the real reason I stood in front of her house. It was fall and I'd seen pomegranates in my favorite store. I wanted to know if there was still a pomegranate tree in my old backyard.

I know every childhood has troubles. I look back and it seems always to have been summer. My bedroom window looked out on the pomegranate tree, visible in moonlight. From my brother's room, I heard his stereo playing the Beatles' *Revolver*, then *Sgt. Pepper's Lonely Hearts Club Band*. Finally, one August, night after night, he played *Magical Mystery Tour*. He played "Your Mother Should Know" over and over, as if it were a lullaby.

That summer my grandmother was sick. My mother went every day to the hospital. I was left in a neighbor's care. I grew sullen after a while, prone to fits and crying jags. When it was time to go to the neighbor, I ran and hid under my bed. My mother couldn't figure out what had gotten into me. I think my brother knew.

A child's sadness is so large because he has nothing with which to compare it. He of course has consolations that are in their way equally large. Our pomegranate tree was my consolation. When my mother brought me home from the neighbor I ran through the house into the backyard and climbed into the tree as high as I could go.

My puzzled mother stood below, staring up. "You look like a little bird perched up there. Are you building a nest?"

In late summer the pomegranate's leaves turned bright yellow. The fruit was pale pink to deep red. Of all varieties, I think ours might have been an Eversweet because it produced ripe fruit from August through November. Or perhaps it was one of the varieties that originated in San Diego, like Renan's Sweet, or King. I'm not sure.

So unlike any other fruit, so unto itself, the pomegranate with its secret chambers, glistening seeds, is perfect for a child. It's toylike and eating it is a game. Pomegranates fire the simple imagination. Perhaps that's why they so often figure in religious literature: the myth of Persephone, Queen of the Dead; the Song of Songs, "Thy temples are like pomegranates within thy locks," and "I will give you spiced pomegranate wine."

I knew from Exodus that small pomegranates ornamented the hem of the robe Aaron wore when he entered the Tabernacle. The Exodus story must have played in my mind when I sat in our tree eating pomegranates. The fruit belonged not to my backyard, but to long ago and far away. I must have imagined sand and sun, pyramids, pillars of fire, scenes of terrible justice.

Pomegranates led my imagination to a big foreign world, distant from what confused and scared me. Perhaps that's why I later fell for the romance of travel, the promise that you can leave your troubles behind, that anywhere at all is better than here.

And the little boy who hid in the pomegranate tree did grow up and travel. He's been around the block. He's seen the show. So it seemed a defeat when I in middle age had to return to my home town, where I discovered that the only house I could afford was just a few blocks from the one I grew up in. Maybe luck had nothing to do with it.

I celebrated my first Rosh Hashanah in my new home. Pomegranates, their many seeds, symbolize hope, fertility, prosperity. The usual you'd want from the new Jewish year. At the end of the meal, I offered my guests pomegranates. I broke the fruit into a bowl of water. The seeds sank, the skin floated to the top. I knew that a few blocks away my childhood tree, if it still stood, was heavy with fruit. We are bound to return to many things. Some of them are sweet.

"KIMBERLY'S TEETH ARE large and her face is too broad," Leon said, sipping the last of his coffee from a tiny white cup. "I am not interested in the least. But she persists."

When I met Leon in the early 1980s he was importing enormous French antiques he hoped to sell to La Jolla matrons. He was a handsome, mustached man with jet-black hair and a terrier-like alertness. His French charm didn't move much merchandise, but the saleswomen in the shops near his found him irresistible. They were always dropping by for cups of strong coffee Leon made in the small French pot, *cafetière*, he heated on a hotplate at the back of his store. This was well before Starbucks planted a café on every American corner. Espresso was still exotic. Leon said American coffee was "dis-gus-ting."

Used to ruminative French women, Leon was intimidated by American females. No American woman addled him more than Kimberly, a big-boned and forthright Iowa blonde who owned a travel agency down the street from his store. Kimberly developed a taste for Leon's dark French roast. Before long she was showing up with boxes of imported sugar cubes and tips on cut-rate Acapulco vacations. Whenever I visited Leon to ask how his business was doing, or ask after his sister, whom I'd met in Israel, he complained about Kimberly.

"She thinks she will win. But she won't. *Jamais*. Never. Last week I was with a French girl and, you know, there is nothing better. It is such a pleasure to have a woman undress you with her own hands."

I'd known women who feigned apathy toward men they desired. I'd never known a man whose apathy wasn't sincere. But for several months I didn't pay much attention to Leon. One day when I called, he announced he was engaged to Kimberly.

"We're moving back to Nice. Kimberly wants to live in France. She is selling her travel agency. I am going to import Mexican boots!"

I dropped in on Leon and Kimberly when they were packing up his things. Surrounded by crates, dust on her cheeks, Kimberly wore a big Iowa State University sweatshirt and couldn't keep her hands off Leon. I wondered how she would do in Nice, surrounded by Leon's complicated Algerian-Jewish family. I called Leon after he and Kimberly had settled in France. He grunted when he answered the phone. He said he was cleaning the stove. Kimberly had done something odd to the *cafetière* and it had exploded. "She can't even learn to make coffee."

Kimberly did learn to use a *cafetière* and, through Leon's and his family's fierce tutelage, transformed herself into a proper *bonne bourgeoise*, a thinner, more manicured version of her former Iowan self. When I finally saw her in Nice she wore trim Chanel suits. She was taking drawing lessons at an art school while Leon introduced Mexican footwear to the Côte d'Azur.

I remember the night was tropical, and their apartment had big sliding-glass doors that looked out on the Mediterranean. We had dinner—fish Kimberly had poached, a salad of bitter greens. Leon went to bed early. Kimberly brought coffee on a tray to the living room where we settled on wide leather couches. She dropped a sugar cube into her cup and stirred it, coffee aroma heavy in the air.

"Did Leon tell you about our trip to Morocco? It was after my miscarriage. We needed to get away. Morocco is fabulous. The people are wonderful, very warm. I was surprised that so many of the men looked like Leon. The same coloring. The same eyes. You know, dark. North African. We had a wonderful time. Incredible food. Everyone speaks French. They thought *I* was French. I guess they couldn't hear my accent. Leon and his family *always* hear my accent."

She paused, looked as if she were about to say something important, then dismissed the thought. She excused herself and went to bed. I finished my coffee alone. The following morning I left Nice. I haven't seen Kimberly since. On my desk at home, however, I keep a postcard of a Cézanne, *Femme à la cafetière*, Woman with a Coffee Pot. In the painting a broad-faced woman in a blue dress stares forward as if something weighed on her mind. On the table beside her sit a cup, saucer, spoon, and *cafetière*.

I can imagine the smell of coffee in the broad-faced woman's dark-paneled room, the same smell which, like dark French tobacco, permeates so many French interiors—cafés, restaurants, kitchens. The French were among the first Europeans to drink coffee. In the late seventeenth century, the Turkish Ambassador introduced it to the French nobility, whose fancy ladies screwed up their faces and fluttered their fans when first confronted with cups of the foreign stuff.

"You will never believe it," Leon shouted over the phone, a year or so after I visited him and Kimberly. "She has left me. I was in the hospital with kidney stones and she came and told me she was leaving. She's gone to Morocco. I am certain she's having affairs with Moroccan men."

I heard him puff on one of his ever-present Gitanes.

"I don't think she was ever in love with me at all."

chapter sixteen

WE ARRIVED IN ISTANBUL in the evening, when the damp Bosporus air blended with the city's sooty haze, yielding a graphite-colored fog. Istanbul burns oil for heat. The fog had a grimy, sulfurous odor that stayed in the nose and permeated our sweaters and over-coats. This fog persisted until late morning so that, bit by bit, as the sun burned through the gray, the city was revealed to us.

Across from our hotel, phantoms moving swiftly about the park turned out to be schoolboys playing soccer. The "castle" down the street was the blocky Russian embassy, guarded by soldiers with polished automatic weapons. The fog retreated further and, in the distance, we could see the Great Mosque's minarets.

My friend Ron and I went to Istanbul because the airfare was reasonable and because Ron was born in the city. He'd lived there till he was five. He hadn't returned for thirty years. We wanted to visit Istanbul's Jewish community, which once was one of the largest in that part of the world. In the fifteenth century Turkey welcomed the Jews that Spain had expelled and, for hundreds of years, their life in Istanbul was good.

Walking down the street, I saw ethnic types I didn't recognize: very tall people with high cheekbones; short, ruddy-faced people who looked like Inuit. Who were they? Ron didn't know. And he couldn't ask. He said he remembered no Turkish. As soon as we'd arrived, he'd slipped into dreamy silence. In an ancient Jewish part of Istanbul we visited a Jewish home for the elderly. Many of the residents seemed to speak not only Turkish and Ladino, a dialect of Hebrew and Spanish, but also Italian.

Italian?

"Because," one eighty-year-old explained, "my cousin married an Italian."

I wanted to tell Ron about this, but couldn't find him. He was on the rest home's top floor, staring out a window.

On the fourth day of our trip a Muslim extremist assassinated one of Turkey's most famous journalists. We were visiting the offices of a Jewish newspaper when we heard the news.

The paper's pretty editor had just explained to us in French that, yes, of course, Turkish Jews enjoyed complete religious and political freedom. While the editor expounded on this freedom, her secretary methodically proceeded to let down all the window blinds and turn off all the lights.

That night there were many roadblocks throughout the city. Police stopped our taxi several times. They scrutinized our passports. Ron and I ended up at a restaurant so traditional it had an upstairs area for unaccompanied women. The menu was in Turkish. Our waiter spoke no English. Ron stared at the menu. He suddenly said "*Visne.*" The waiter nodded, walked away, and returned with a glass of ruby red liquid. "Cherry juice," Ron explained. "I drank it as a child." He looked again at the menu. "*Patlican.* That's eggplant." A few seconds later, "*Nohut.* That means garbanzo beans."

The "cherry juice" that tripped a switch in Ron's mind was likely made from a *surup*, or syrup, of the kind introduced to Turkey by the Muslim conquest. Turks learned to use fruit syrups to make drinks and, in the summer, sherbets. Eighteenth century British who ventured into the Ottoman world were particularly fascinated by these sherbets and syrups, by the notion of voluptuous Turkish women lounging in bathhouses, sipping fruit juices while slave girls braided their hair.

I think the syrups stay in the mind because they have an intense perfume. The cherry syrup I keep in my kitchen smells strongly of ripe cherries. Its flavor is sharp, sweet, a little sour.

This flavor, this aroma, turned Ron into a Turkish chatterbox. After his first sip of cherry juice, he began to utter Turkish nouns and phrases. He started to read street signs aloud.

His parents' marriage had not been a happy one. They divorced not long after they left Istanbul. Ron still had an aunt who lived in the city. She threw her arms around his neck when she saw him. She wept. She offered us cherry juice. She fed us breast of chicken smothered in walnut sauce. She, like most Turkish Jews, felt great loyalty to Turkey and was very nationalistic. When we mentioned the smelly fog she clucked and told us, "Istanbul has the cleanest air in the world."

When it came time to leave Istanbul, Ron left with regret, although, he said, his childhood had not been happy there. On the morning we left, we stood in front of our hotel waiting for a taxi. There was a cold strong wind from the east that swept the fog away. From where we stood we could see, for once, clearly across the park. To Ron's surprise we could see on the park's far side the building where he had lived as a child.

chapter seventeen

W HEN I WAS SEVENTEEN, already hirsute, and living in Japan, I went on a school trip to Kyushu, the archipelago's southeastern island. On the first night, I and sixty Japanese boys jostled into our inn's communal bath for a long soak in the swimming-pool-size tub. I had just tucked my boxers into a little plastic basket when one of my classmates approached me and tugged the curly black hair on my chest.

"*Ara!*" he said. "*Gorira mitai ya na!*" ("Hey, you look like a gorilla!")

He was a Kyoto boy, from a rough part of town, and he'd never before seen a naked white boy, much less a hairy one. He spoke with a lurid southern accent. What he said actually sounded more like, "Hey, ya'll look like a gorilla, dontch' ye?"

Everyone roared. He chuckled, slapped my fuzzy ass, "*Keito!*"

Keito, hairy barbarian, is the Japanese pejorative for white person. The nickname stuck, and through some process of racial transmigration followed me, years later, to a local Japanese restaurant where I worked as a sushi chef's assistant. The chef's name was Takegawa. The restaurant's name was Miki-San. For a while in the early '80s it was popular with Japanese businessmen whom Takegawa delighted by calling me *keito*, to which he added the superlative honorific suffix -*sama*. I was "*keito-sama.*"

"Honorable Mr. Hairy Barbarian, I need more squid!"

"Honorable Mr. Hairy Barbarian, bring me another glass of vodka!"

Takegawa drank like a fish while wielding his sharp sushi knives. One of my tasks was to fetch his drinks from the bar. Another was to scrub and clean the day's cold rubbery octopus. Another was to rinse and pat dry the green fuzzy *shiso* leaves on which Takegawa arranged his opalescent slices of sashimi.

Shiso, or perilla, is a member of the mint family, and like some varieties of mint and its relatives, *shiso* is covered with small fine hairs botanists call "pubescence." If you take a *shiso* leaf into your mouth, you can feel this faint roughness against your tongue. *Shiso*'s taste is unusual, meaty, a little like basil, and while I worked at the sushi bar I'd snack on a few leaves if Takegawa wasn't looking. When I left work, I'd slip a dozen leaves into my pocket and drive out to the beach where, smelling of raw fish, I'd sit on a jetty, chew *shiso*, stare at the roiling sea, and reminiscence about Japan.

I had been happy there where I'd ruined my eyes by spending long nights studying Japanese characters, copying out hundreds of them by hand. You need to know about 1800 characters to read a newspaper. By the time I left Japan I doubt if I knew more than 800, most of which had been taught to me by Michiko, a high-school senior who'd volunteered to tutor me in exchange for English lessons. Michiko was Protestant, a rarity in Japan, and I think she felt some kinship with my foreignness. On late afternoons, while her watchful mother padded about the kitchen, we built our respective vocabularies with thick piles of flashcards. Once a week, her mother served us dinner, which often as not included small slices of raw tuna wrapped in leaves of *shiso*.

I of course repaid this woman's generosity by sleeping with her daughter. The act was accomplished in an apartment that belonged to a friend of Michiko, a French teacher who'd gone to Lyons for the summer. Michiko and I grappled on the tatami. Outside, cicadas droned. Inside, mosquitoes skittered about the ceiling's corners. Sweat stung my eyes. I worried that I smelled bad: some Japanese complain that white people stink like rancid butter. (They have a point. Caucasian armpits are spongy with sweat glands, of which the Japanese have comparatively few.) My judo coach had once ordered me home to wash my uniform. He claimed it "stank of foreigner." If Michiko thought I smelled bad, she said nothing.

My hairy body, I think, pleased and repelled her. Sex itself was new to her, and sex with a boy who looked so foreign could have been only doubly strange. I recall being surprised by the clarity of her sweat-slick skin. As teenagers, we didn't so much make love as tussle in a clumsy parody of sex. We knew too little for it to be pleasurable. She bled. We weren't after pleasure, anyway. We were after thrill, the chilly forbidden. I know that I, grunting, clambered on top of her because I wanted to. I was too young to realize that it's perhaps not good to always take what one wants.

We uncoupled and lay panting, our wet backs sticking to the tatami. I felt, I remember, very far from home. Michiko sat upright, drew her knees to her chest, and began to weep. The cicadas pulsed beyond the windows. I put my arm around her. She pushed me away, "*Dame ya!*" No.

Even in the back of my hormone-addled brain, I realized I had lost a friend. I maybe even sensed it was somehow more complicated than that. I sat beside her and rubbed my kneecaps, crosshatched in red from kneeling on tatami. Michiko hid her face with one hand and continued to cry. With her other hand she caressed the hair on my forearm.

I'M READING FROM *Eating Together: Recollections & Recipes*, a culinary memoir by Lillian Hellman and Peter Feibleman, her sometime lover and perpetual confidante. Feibleman says, "Coast to coast, almost any rice recipe you pick up will tell you in the strictest terms that cooked rice must be dry, white and fluffy. Forget it. In New Orleans, as in India and other countries where rice is considered a staple, people would just as soon have it moist, colorful, and gummy."

As Feibleman's comment suggests, *Eating Together* isn't reliable. Feibleman and Hellman boozed together, and their recipes and "cooking tips" imply a lot of yelling and fumbling in a hot kitchen, bourbon or Burgundy in hand, trying to remember if the pot roast was shoved into the oven an hour ago or yesterday afternoon. I mention *Eating Together* only to show that even the most obscure cook like Feibleman holds strong opinions about rice.

Almost everywhere rice is eaten, people are said to have elevated its cooking to an art form. No other staple radiates as many taboos and ritualistic strictures. Claudia Roden's *A Book of Middle Eastern Food* lists four basic ways of cooking plain white rice, while admitting that throughout the Middle East, "Each family cherishes a particular method and is skeptical about all others, refusing to believe that it is possible to achieve successful results in any way other than their own." In Shizuo Tsuji's *Japanese Cooking: A Simple Art*, a classic text, the author's rice-cooking instructions occupy five full pages: "Cover rice with cold water from the tap and stir quickly with your hands for about thirty seconds, till the water becomes milky. Never let the rice stand in this milky water. . . . Pour off milky water and wash again with fresh water from the tap. Repeatedly wash this way until water is *almost* clear. It takes about five minutes of washing, pouring off, and washing to clean rice sufficiently. The penalty for rice washed too hastily is 'smelly' rice. Stir more gently in later washings than at first in order not to bruise grains. . . ." A simple art, indeed.

Bruised grains. Smelly rice. Wash it five times. Wash it six times. Don't wash it. I remember my father's wiry older sister screaming at anyone who interrupted her while she stirred her *orez nabusit prajit*, a kind of Romanian risotto, "You're going to make me ruin this!" It's a wonder my hands don't shake when I pour a cupful of Mahatma brand extra long grain enriched rice into a pot of boiling water. (Even my trusty Mahatma brand can't help being bossy. "TO RETAIN VITAMINS," reads the package, "DO NOT RINSE BEFORE OR DRAIN AFTER COOKING.")

All this language couched in the imperative, like the Thou-shalts and Thou-shalt-nots heard by hungry Moses on Sinai. There's plaintiveness to these rice commandments, an echo of times when rice and water were the only things that stood between you and a long grinding slide into ravenous eternity. Respect rice, or else.

I learned many rice commandments when I was young and

living in Japan and too uneducated and too superficial to devote much thought to why people observed customs. I did as I was told. Always finish your rice. Always compliment your hostess on her rice. Never jab your chopsticks vertically into your rice bowl and leave them there because that's done only to a bowl of rice at funerals. In the Kyoto family with whom I lived each person had his or her own pair of chopsticks and his or her own rice bowl. You never traded them or swapped them and they were yours and yours alone until you left the household or died.

We're going back decades. Who knows if this custom is observed anymore? Snow was falling on Kyoto and in the hills outside the city when a very old member of the family I was living with died. I remember a long walk up a narrow road, snow crunching under my shoes. I remember a traditional Kyoto home, maybe a century old, whose living room was draped entirely, ceiling and walls, in white cloth. A pine coffin sat at the front of the room. A small table sat before the coffin and on it was a blue rice bowl filled with rice. Two black chopsticks had been thrust vertically into the dome of fluffy grains.

Legs tucked beneath us on the chilly tatami, we each took turns dropping incense onto a tray of charcoal embers. We bowed our heads, palms pressed together in respect. We returned the next morning—these traditional Kyoto funerals were a long affair. I didn't know the many mourners. I didn't know the ninety-year-old woman who had died. What I do know is that on the snowy morning we returned, our breath cottony-white in the air, the family observed a very old Kyoto custom. When the coffin was carried from the house, the dead woman's oldest daughter stood in the doorway holding her mother's rice bowl. After the coffin crossed the threshold, the daughter dashed the bowl to the ground—a sharp and indelible sound in the winter morning air. At that moment, the first time in a night and day of mourning, I heard people cry.

chapter eighteen

THE PACT THEY MADE was the commonplace pact of men and women in those days. A half-century later, Marty shuffles behind Hannah as they usher their pact to conclusion.

I think about that duo while I grate hard-boiled eggs into a big green bowl of chopped liver. My fingers smell of blood and raw onions. My hair and beard have the sugary-sweet slightly sulfurous smell of onions fried dark brown. Every Passover, Hannah makes sure that Sue and I sit near her and Marty at the seder. Hannah describes all single people as "alone."

"No one," she says, "should sit alone at a seder."

Last year after I spent all day making chopped liver, my usual contribution to the occasion, I sat beside Hannah. She jabbed me with her elbow.

"No wonder you can't find a new wife," she whispered. "You smell like a delicatessen."

I'd spent the day frying cupfuls of onion in fragrant chicken fat. I grilled pounds of kosher chicken livers in my oven. Inky blood dripped from the livers and with a hiss hit the pan beneath them. Disconsolate smoke hovered above the stove. Blood is a pervasive taboo.

In Jewish law it's blood that makes a woman periodically unavailable to her husband. A speck of blood in a fresh egg renders it *treyf*, unkosher. Blood is the reason we scatter coarse salt onto freshly slaughtered meat: salt draws blood to the surface where we rinse it away. Liver is a bloody organ and requires special treatment. It must be grilled so that its blood may drip away. I endure the fuss because Sue loves my chopped liver.

We've known each other for decades. Since my divorce, Sue appears one evening each spring at my door. Bright-eyed, beautifully dressed, she drives me to the seder. Each Passover she's excited, eager, and pretty. Each year at this time I think we ask ourselves why we don't, in a fit of pragmatic optimism, marry each other.

Sue knocks at my front door. I hand her my green bowl of chopped liver. A visceral oniony smell rises from the bowl. It's

an intimate odor, a *bodily* odor. It introduces a carnal awareness to our otherwise asexual greeting.

"My, oh, my," Sue giggles. She handles the bowl gingerly.
"This smells *good*, but I think I'll put it in the trunk."

We are two of fourteen guests. As soon as we arrive we're
absorbed into the seder's multilingual hubbub. There are
Israeli chemists and Yiddish-speaking Polish Jews from
Mexico City and Turkish Jews from Mexico City and English-
only American Jews. Polyglot children and a yellow Labrador
scramble around the table. Our very pregnant hostess stands
in the kitchen, absently rubbing her belly. Her Turkish-
Mexican husband pours wine for everyone. I sit beside
Hannah. Sue, beside Marty. The seder begins.

We read aloud about lamb's blood smeared over slave-hut
doors to ward off the Death Angel. We read that the Nile
turned to blood. We sing about frogs and blood and burning
hail. On the seder plate, the burned lamb shank, boiled egg,
parsley, horseradish, matzo, salt water, apples cooked with
walnuts, tell a story. Everyone commemorates the Exodus
except Marty. He's had so many strokes, his memory's so
filled with holes, that Hannah says his brain looks like
"Swiss cheese."

"Sometimes he even thinks I'm his sister."

Finally it's time for dinner. Around the table we pass gefilte
fish and my chopped liver. Hannah takes a healthy serving.

"It's good for a man to cook," she says, looking at me but
talking to Sue. "It makes things more even."

Hannah winks at me. Marriage. For Hannah the world is one big wedding.

"I was never a good cook," Hannah says. "My mother never taught me. Right after we were married, Marty asked me to make stew. What's a stew? I remembered that in my mother's stew the vegetables floated. So, I thought, in stew the food should *float*. And what makes things *float*? Water. So, I kept adding water. And more water. But the carrots and onions and meat kept sinking. I kept adding more water. It all finally cooked down to this mush, this glop. Not even a dog would eat it. Not even Marty."

Hannah wipes matzo crumbs from Marty's lips. He stares at her, unseeing.

We work our way through chicken soup, brisket, glazed carrots, potato kugel, another glass of wine. We clear the table and pass plates of halvah, Turkish delight, coconut macaroons.

Hannah sips her decaf. She looks at Sue. She looks at me. She's been waiting all evening for this moment.

"Why don't the two of you get married?"

Ruddy and giddy with Passover wine, Sue rises unsteadily from the table. "I think I need a little glass of water."

Hannah watches her go. "She's a very nice girl. But, let's face it, no spring chicken."

She pats my shoulder. "Neither are you."

Guests search for coats. Marty feeds the Labrador a piece of matzo. Fathers with drowsy kids slung over their shoulders wander toward the front door. I hear Sue laughing in the kitchen.

Marty slaps both hands on the table, gazes at the ceiling.

"That stew," he says in a loud voice. "My God, that stew was awful. Terrible! The worst thing I've ever tasted."

Hannah smiles. She cups his raspy chin in her palm.

"After fifty years, he can't even remember his own name." She kisses his mouth. "After fifty years the only thing he remembers is my stew."